The Politics
of
Expert Advice

Creating, Using and Manipulating
Scientific Knowledge for Public Policy

Edited by
ANTHONY BARKER
and
B. GUY PETERS

UNIVERSITY OF PITTSBURGH PRESS

Published in the USA by the University of Pittsburgh Press,
Pittsburgh, Pa. 15260

© Edinburgh University Press, 1993

Typeset in Monotype Times New Roman
by Combined Arts, Edinburgh, and
printed in Great Britain by
The University Press, Cambridge

LC 92–64446

A CIP record for this book is available from the Library of Congress

ISBN 0–8229–1171–X

ISBN 0–8229–6098–2 (pbk)

Fellowship, Michaelmas Term, 1989); the Rockefeller Foundation (Resident Scholar appointment, Conference and Study Center, Villa Serbelloni, Bellagio, Lake Como, 1990); St John's College, Oxford (Summer Visiting Scholar 1989); and the Department of Government, University of Essex (Research Endowment Fund).

We both would like to thank the editorial and production team at Edinburgh University Press and offer warm appreciation to June Mead of 'Laserprint', Wivenhoe, Essex, who typed the successive versions of both volumes' chapters on to disk with great patience and stamina.

Acknowledgements

This book concerning the theme of advice for public policy-makers in advanced Western political systems is published by Edinburgh University Press as one of a pair. Particulars of the other volume are listed at the back of this book for the convenience of interested readers, who will find it useful to see both books because they have been devised to complement each other. One is mainly concerned with the processes and institutions for conveying advice to governments while the other concentrates on the particular problems of doing this in policy fields of great technical difficulty, such as medicine, science and advanced technology.

We cordially acknowledge the European Consortium for Political Research (based in the Department of Government at the University of Essex) as the original forum for two of the eight chapters in this present volume *The Politics of Expert Advice: Creating, Using and Manipulating Scientific Knowledge for Public Policy*. Every year, this unique association of some 150 academic departments and in-stitutes of political science in Western Europe brings together several hundred scholars and advanced students to form a wide array of research workshops where research papers are discussed. One of these was devised and organized by Anthony Barker on the theme of advice for policy-making in Western European states. We are grateful to these workshop collaborators for their chapters, as also to the authors of the chapters which we have arranged to add, thus making two books adopting somewhat different approaches to this very broad theme. Our particular thanks as editors are due to Richard Topf, who has followed up his workshop membership with a Conclusion chapter for each book which he has prepared in the light of our Introduction and the other chapters.

Anthony Barker wishes to acknowledge the generous support during his writing and editing work for this volume of Fitzwilliam College, Cambridge (Visiting

Contents

Notes on Contributors

ANTHONY BARKER is a Reader in the Department of Government at the University of Essex. He has been Visiting Professor in the Department of Political Science, University of Wisconsin at Madison (1986–7): a senior Simon Fellow at The University of Manchester (1983); a Visiting Fellow of Fitzwilliam College, Cambridge (1989) and a Resident Scholar at The Rockefeller Foundation's Study Center, Bellagio, Italy (1990). Book publications include *The MP and his Information* (with Michael Rush), *Public Property and Private Interests: The Institutions of Compromise* (joint editor with Douglas Hague and W.J.M. MacKenzie), *Quangos in Britain* (editor) and the companion to this present volume (particulars of which appear elsewhere in this volume). Apart from the theme of information and advice in public policy-making, he has a special interest in professional roles in public affairs, notably in land-use planning.

B. GUY PETERS is Maurice Falk Professor of American Government and Chair of the Department of Political Science at the University of Pittsburgh. He has been a Fulbright Professor at the University of Strathclyde and at the Hochschule St Gallen (Switzerland) and was Hallsworth Fellow of Political Economy at the University of Manchester. Professor Peters has written a number of books on public policy and administration including *The Politics of Taxation: A Comparative Perspective, European Politics Reconsidered* and *Comparing Public Bureaucracies*. He is also the co-editor of *Governance*. His current research mainly concerns policy formulation and comparative institutional reform.

ANGELA LIBERATORE is a research assistant at the European University Institute in Florence. She has published in the *European Journal of Political*

Research on environmental policy in the EC. Current interests include the EC context of global environmental risks. She acknowledges the co-operation of the Ministry of Civil Protection, ENEA, ENEA-DISP and ISS in Italy while preparing her chapter, which is linked to her EUI Ph.D. thesis on the impact of 'Chernobyl' in Italy, Germany and France and the EC's policy system in Brussels.

SALLY MACGILL specialized for many years in political and social research into the human impact of radioactive discharges, as a member of the School of Geography at the University of Leeds. She is now that university's Planning Officer. She is author of *The Politics of Anxiety: Sellafield's cancer-link controversy* and joint author of *Scientific Reassurance as Public Policy: The logic of the Black Report.*

CHRISTINE MIRONESCO is a member of the Department of Political Science at the University of Geneva. She has a long-standing research interest in the politics of nuclear power in Switzerland.

WOLFGANG RÜDIG is a Senior Lecturer in the Department of Government at the University of Strathclyde, Glasgow. He is the author of *Anti-Nuclear Movements: A world survey of opposition to nuclear energy* and co-author of *The Green Wave: A comparative analysis of ecological parties.* He is also editor of the *Green Politics* annual volumes and the Environment, Politics and Society series (both from Edinburgh University Press).

MICHAEL SAWARD is a Lecturer in Public Administration at Royal Holloway and Bedford New College, University of London. His publications include *Co-optive Politics and State Legitimacy.* Current interests are problems in democratic theory and the concept of policy networks.

JEAN TOURNON is Chargé de Récherche at the National Foundation of Political Sciences, University of Grenoble. He has published on France's public authorities as France's principal lobbying group (in *Jean Méynaud, or the Utopian Dream Revisited*) and on ethnicity in the emerging federal Western Europe (in journals and as conference papers).

RICHARD TOPF is a Principal Lecturer in Politics at the City of London Polytechnic and a Member of Nuffield College, Oxford. Current work includes comparisons of British, German and Swedish political cultures and membership of the Beliefs in Government research project (supported by the European Science Foundation). Among his numerous publications is *British Political Culture* (forthcoming). Research interests include theories of the State as well as political cultures and participation.

One

Introduction
Science Policy and Government

ANTHONY BARKER AND B. GUY PETERS

POLICY DIFFICULTIES AND SCIENTIFIC ADVICE

The purpose of this volume is to consider the place of technical, expert advice to government in official decision-making in technically difficult and sophisticated policy fields. All public policy fields in all political systems require expertise of some kind because they contain much detail and usually complexity. Some fields are not merely elaborate in their detail but also complicated, so that various concepts, rules or systematic distinctions are needed if much sense is to be made of the material on display. Some fields may be more or less elaborate or complicated but are a further challenge to the observer because they are technically difficult and sophisticated: only people who have studied or trained in the field can hope to understand the substantive material. Within these technically difficult policy fields, some are innately very hard to understand, perhaps because a great deal of scientific, mathematical or statistical background is needed. A few policy fields are exceptionally hard to grasp because they turn on technical questions which, as yet, have no generally known and accepted scientific answers. Not only the layman policy-maker but the scientific experts themselves lack the knowledge which is needed to solve a policy problem or to manage a policy field according to some chosen course.

If an example of each of these levels of difficulty is taken from (say) the health care field, we may make a list such as is shown in Figure 1.1.

Tasks arising in groups (i) to (iii) offer no real mystery to the lay policy-maker who is prepared to spend time and effort studying the problems which they raise. Policy-makers such as health ministers, senior administrative officials and members of health or hospital boards and commissions who wish to invest their time

Figure 1.1.   Six levels of cognitive difficulty in public policy fields

	Policy field's character	Possible examples in health care
(i)	*Elaborate detail*	The organization and monitoring of community doctors, and other medical services' records and routine provision.
(ii)	*Complexity*	Organization and monitoring of hospital services or the supply of different types of nursing care.
(iii)	*Technical difficulty* but – like (i) and (ii) – amenable to non-expert study.	Priority distribution of scarce resources such as kidney machines; operating theatre use; health care budgets and building programs.
(iv)	*Technical difficulty* which those with expert training (e.g.epidemiological data or probabilistic mathematics, statistics,analysis of future health care needs; economics, medicine) can appreciate and judge.	Strategic budget plans based on epidemiological data or probabalistic analysis of future health care needs: cost-benefit studies of potential health care priorities or possible costing exercises on (e.g.) road accidents or drug addiction's burden on the health service.
(v)	*Technical difficulty* bordering on the scientifically unknown, and with rival and controversial scientific views on offer.	Various claimed cures, reliefs, vaccines, etc. for important diseases or conditions; various medical strategies for coping with major health threats such as AIDS, drug addiction or degenerative conditions among the elderly.
(vi)	*Scientifically unknown:* no rival claims from experts.	Diseases (such as Alzheimer's or Parkinson's) with no known treatment or cure and no claims yet entered by medical researchers.

can have matters explained to them fully by the administrators or financial managers more immediately involved. There is scope for advisers or consultants at this simpler level of problem analysis, but they are not analytical experts so much as operational ones. They can be used to establish and measure the empirical details of the problem or the field in question. They can run surveys, make sample checks or conduct case studies. Their services may well be a worthwhile investment in drafting some new and reformist administrative scheme for community doctors' surgeries or hospital patients' appointments. At this level of work these consultants may claim prior experience in equivalent large-scale administrative systems such as public sector fields other than health care or in commercial fields such as retailing. Such large-scale, computer-based operations as keeping many supermarkets or other large stores supplied with innumerable different lines of goods in exactly the right way to avoid either shortages or over-stocking have much in common with major hospitals admitting and treating a variety of patients. Of course, the stakes are higher because the political and moral cost of the hospital failing to treat an emergency case for lack of immediately available staff or supplies does not arise from a particular local shop's failure to offer some desired item. So, resource planning and the search for 'efficiency' in the public and private sectors will always be different, even under political masters who continually urge commercial and market approaches on to the managers of health care, education, social work, police or other public services.

The ideas of administrative consultants at this level are usually pretty elementary and clear essays in rational methods, self-monitoring (feedback) cost controls and so on, which the supervising policy-makers can understand and judge. The main service performed for them by their own in-house administrators or by outside consultants is to illustrate the current facts and the problems arising, followed by implementation of some reformist scheme. The 'working' of this calculation can be followed by policy-makers who are willing to make the effort. There is no secret material or opaque calculations which remain inside a 'black box' whose operation the policy-maker must either take on trust or simply reject. Expert advisers, whether in-house or out-of-house, can be made to explain every step in their work – at least, if the decision-makers so insist and if time permits.

Where policy-makers face issues of types (iv) to (vi) the advisory process is different. Mere elaborateness, largeness, complexity or fairly simple technical difficulty are surpassed. Real technical difficulties now overshadow these other characteristics, although these others may still form part of the field and the problem in question. Thus, in the health field for example, the range of different kinds of cancer or heart disease combines with the variety of types of sufferers to produce a complicated field, although these matters are overshadowed by the medical uncertainty and controversy surrounding at least some types of cancer treatment. At these levels, the medical experts cannot explain themselves fully to their laymen employers. If the experts agree, they must rely on their united qualified opinions to carry the day. If they disagree, they can only compete with rival experts in getting their view of some technical issue accepted. Only the exceptional policy-maker has specialist training to follow the language and techniques involved in a full expert explanation and, even then, probably only in part. At the highest levels of technical difficulty, the experts cannot claim to know enough to create a scientific consensus or even to maintain a fairly stable scientific difference of opinion. Types (v) and (vi) of policy issue cross the borders of current scientific knowledge. Any policy based on some particular view or guess as to the facts of the matter would be speculative. It may be acceptable to try such a shot in the dark because it would generate some actual experience of the problem or further research, or because political pressure requires decision-makers to do something (anything) about the problem in question. But, at the level of the unknown, expert advice of the usual kind, based on experience, knowledge and reasoning, is no longer available – although the different services of policy ideologues, enthusiasts, visionaries and seers may well be (O'Riordan *et al.* 1988).

Thus, one task facing any systematic attempt to analyze the role of expert advice in public policy-making is to distinguish different levels and types of advice-giving – and of the expertise lying behind it – which are suitable for different levels of policy-making difficulty. This includes recognizing when experts are speaking from a near-consensus (of general methods or assumptions, if not also of particular conclusions on cases) as opposed to their being seriously divided among themselves on these things. Finally, students of policy-making (and, of course, policy-makers themselves) should recognize when there is no expertise to be had, at least for the time being. Policy-makers have a dangerous tendency to pretend that they have access to usable scientific advice when, on some matters, they actually do not. This tendency is closely associated with the general sense of omnicompetence which attaches to public policy-makers, not least in those democratic systems where they are accountable to legislatures, the mass media or to public opinion. There is often a vain hope of maintaining the myth that all problems and issues are safely under their hand, usually with the help of expert advisers.

An understanding of the different levels of certainty in policy advice should prompt the use of different modes of decision. If there is agreement and virtual scientific certainty, then rather straightforward decision-making can be trusted. When there is greater uncertainty, models which include risk in the analysis should be used (Rubenstein 1975). In the most extreme cases, policy-making becomes, in Dror's (1983) term, 'policy gambling', with little *a priori* knowledge of the costs and benefits of a decision. At times such gambling may be necessary, but it can still incorporate the best scientific advice available.

This six-part list takes health care as its field because this very varied field contains the full range of characteristics from the simplest examples of elementary rational administration to problems such as 'incurable' diseases which lie beyond present scientific skills. Several of the chapters in this book concern this top end of the scale – types (v) or (vi) – including currently unsolved mysteries such as the genetic damage which is caused by radioactivity and which produces child leukaemias. By contrast, there is little or no political science or policy analysis interest in the elementary challenges represented by types (i) or (ii) – the elaborate, complex, but transparent administrative issues.

THE CONVENTIONAL WISDOM ABOUT SCIENCE

The world of the late twentieth century is dominated by science and technology. These twin pillars of the modern world have the capacity both for great good and for great harm. Further, they and their power have placed great demands on government for control and for support and the most interesting issues about science are now 'trans-science' issues (Weinberg 1972a). That is, they are issues that science itself cannot resolve, and that require the involvement of some other power – most often government. Trans-science issues arise in part because science is not so uniform and orderly as is often believed by the lay person, and in part because of the effects of science and technology on the rest of society. This book will raise many of these issues and demonstrate how they have been dealt with in several industrialized democracies. The 'answers' which arise for issues of science and technology in these cases are largely suggestive, but they do indicate some of the issues and some of the options available to governments.

The conventional wisdom about science is that it is a well-ordered and progressive system of knowledge. Such a view was well illustrated in Thomas Kuhn's

(1962) idea of 'normal science' and this view of scientists' linear progress disturbed only by major scientific revolutions is popular. In addition, the conventional wisdom about science is built on a clear dichotomy between facts and values. It is assumed that science can determine a fact, that facts represent an objective reality and that values or beliefs play no role in the determination of facts. In addition, science presents its practitioners with the puzzles that need to be solved; science is not (and should not be) concerned with changing social, economic and political fashions. In this view, science is a closed system of discovery, relatively impervious to the fashions of the world, and thrives through this very insulation from other concerns and other potential sources of knowledge (Grove 1989). The problem with this simplistic view of science is that it is wrong, or at least it is seriously incomplete and unidimensional (Howson and Urbach 1989; Fischer 1990).

In the first place, the 'fact' in science is a much more fragile item than most lay persons (or even many scientists) are willing to accept. Most facts are, in reality, determined by theory and by the particular measurements of the observer. As such, they have little meaning outside of a system of theories and conventions. Kuhn pointed this out with respect to scientific revolutions, but it should be understood as a more general characteristic of scientific enquiry. Even very simple 'facts' depend upon concepts and measurement. Water boils at 100 C, but this depends upon a concept (temperature) and a measuring scale (centigrade). As we move from simple and agreed facts like boiling water, the dependence of fact upon theory and technique (and therefore upon the values of the observer) becomes even more crucial (Macgill, in this volume).

At an even more extreme level, it can be argued that 'facts' cannot exist independent of theory. The natural world (much less the world constructed by humans) is an extremely complex system. Without some guidance coming from theory, or from other organizing principles for knowledge, meaningful observations are virtually impossible. Even early naturalistic enquiry of a Linnean variety required a notion of classification into which the species observed could be placed. As science has progressed to deal with increasingly complex subject matter, the theoretical element in observation has increased and the pure factual element has been decreased. Therefore, without such a system, there can be little usable knowledge and hence the notion of a fact distinct from theories and values makes little sense. And, if that is the case, then claims of total objectivity on the part of science are not compelling.

It is also important to note the extent to which competition and conflict exists within science. Rather than there being one scientific reality there may be several, each vying with the others for dominance. This competition may be internal to science, but it also has a public element as well. The competition may be for the most attention and the most money, from public sources and the mass media. Again, this means that there cannot logically be one scientific reality and one set of scientific facts. This, in turn, means that scientific advice on public policy issues may be – and almost always should be – conflicting. This would not make the job of government any easier, but it would reflect the reality of science and the reality of the social and physical world. Those who depend upon science and technology for 'the answer' are very likely to be disappointed.

PUBLIC INVOLVEMENT AND CONTROL

The above scepticism about science should be seen as making public intervention in scientific issues more justifiable and more desirable. Indeed, the 'trans-science' nature of many issues requires that the public be involved and that science to some extent becomes more responsible to the public. This is by no means a plea to create an 'official science' of some sort. Rather, it is a statement of the important public interest issues involved in science and technology. Those issues arise for at least three reasons.

Expense and expanse

Firstly, science and technology is expensive and is becoming even more so. This is obviously true for 'big science' projects such as high-energy physics and radio astronomy, but is now increasingly true for more modest areas such as biology and basic chemistry. The need to build laboratories, hire technicians and fund experiments drives the cost of science increasingly high. Even the social sciences have experienced some increase in costs as more large-scale programmes of research are proposed. For the public sector the increasing costs of science are a problem because government is expected to pay a large portion of the bill. Following from that, it can be argued that if government is expected to pay, it should also have some role in determining the priorities of science and can make claims on the scientific establishment for assistance with social needs. Again, this is not a call for a prescribed mode of inquiry, only for a closer link between the public sector and the establishment governing science.

Risk

A second reason for a significant public role in science and technology is that the development of science, especially technology, imposes risks on the public. This is not to be a book on risk analysis: that field is already well analyzed in other books (Douglas and Wildavsky 1982; Douglas 1985). Rather, we merely point to the need to consider the real risks of scientific projects and their subsequent applications on the public. Governments have a well-established obligation to protect the safety and health of their citizens and to allow technical progress to go unconsidered would violate that obligation. The risks to citizens from science have been clearest in areas such as nuclear power and chemical production (Macgill, Liberatore and Saward, in this volume) but also arise in areas such as genetic research and food additives. Therefore, governments again may have a significant role to play in imposing their power between their citizens and the risks which may be imposed upon those citizens. No regulatory regime can be foolproof, but there is generally sufficient knowledge available to reduce collective risk.

Priority setting

The final consideration arguing for a greater public sector role in science is that the mechanisms for priority setting and resource allocation may not reflect the needs of the society at large. First, there may not be a desirable balance between pure science and technological application. In some instances there may be scientific discoveries but little application, with the basic infrastructure needed to support the application allowed to erode. Neither of these imbalances is healthy and there may be a need for public intervention to correct them. Finding the best balance may be difficult, but the issue should be ventilated and some attempt made to try to achieve balance. That ventilation is less likely to happen without a significant role for the public sector in setting science and research policy.

Another concern about the priorities of science, related to the first, is that 'big science' may dominate smaller and less glamorous projects. Big science can be seen in projects such as CERN and JET and in the competition over the location of a new synchrotron machine in Europe (Tournon, in this volume) and a particle accelerator in the United States. These projects cost huge sums of public money. They are certainly valuable, but it is not clear whether their value equals what might be achieved through the investment of the same funds in smaller projects. Within the scientific community, however, to question 'big science' approaches heresy and its high priests tend to dominate review bodies and scientific advisory panels. Thus, it is not clear whether science itself would be able to assess the efficiency and opportunity costs of these projects objectively. There may be problems with using government to do the assessing, but there may at least be somewhat greater objectivity.

A CHECK-LIST FOR SCIENCE POLICY CONSTRUCTION

With some idea of the justification for science policies now in mind, we shall discuss a check-list of questions and issues that any industrialized state should consider before taking action in the field. Many of these questions may be asked concerning any policy, not just science policy. Others, however, are directly related to the central role of knowledge and advice in making science policy.

What is the problem?

The first question is a generic question which arises any time there is a policy to be made. This is simply 'what is the problem?' Except in a few highly progressive and planning-oriented societies, government usually does not act unless there is a perceived problem. But public problems do not come to government neatly labelled and a social and political struggle may emerge over the definition of the problem. This is the basic 'social constructivist' perspective on social problems (Schneider 1985) which, like our discussion of the role of theory in defining facts in science, points to the role of underlying value theories in shaping the reality of social and political problems (Fischer 1990).

As well as being an intellectual problem, the definition of an issue is an important political issue as well. The manner in which a problem is defined will determine which organization and which set of experts will have the first and perhaps only opportunity to address the problem. The case of AIDS policy is an excellent example of the way in which a problem can be captured by one set of experts to the exclusion of other contenders. The problem was defined initially as a technical problem of an unknown virus, and hence was placed in the hands of virologists. A cure for the disease became the policy goal. The alternative construction of the problem, as one of social behaviour, which would have placed the problem in the hands of public health and social work experts, was not considered until much later. The failure to address the behavioural issues in the interim may have allowed many additional people to contract the disease. Although both conceptions of AIDS have some validity, the selection of one placed too much power in the hands of that group of experts (Street 1992). Similar arguments can be made concerning drug policy, economic development and a host of other policies.

The 'issue capturing' that surrounds any innovative issue may be done for the best possible reasons (Dunn 1981). An organization may believe that its resources and methods represents the best way to solve the problem and may aggressively seek to claim it and solve it. This may represent excessive faith in the method used by the organization but it is carried out for sincere and policy-oriented reasons. An organization may, of course, seek to capture a new problem simply to expand its own budget and its own importance (Downs 1967). Most new public problems fall on the boundaries between organizations so that there will be competition to seize those new problems and the new resources that often go with them. There is always the danger that a new problem will become a poisoned chalice for the organizations and produce failure rather than more resources, but most are willing to accept that risk.

Who knows what about the problem?

Just as there may be some question about what the problem really is, there may be some question of whom to consult about it. That problem may be solved to some degree once the problem is defined; certain experts go with certain problem definitions. Even if the problem can be defined unambiguously, there may still be alternative sets of experts who can be summoned. This may represent the competition and diversity within science alluded to earlier. Such diversity and even contradiction is more common when the social sciences are being used as the experts. The changing fashion of economic advice illustrates that point clearly (Singer 1992) and economics is generally cited as the best developed (in scientific terms) of the social sciences. It can occur, however, when the natural sciences' resources are being used. Take, for example, the variety of medical service offered for dealing with the problem of heart disease (Mills – see Topf below) or for the safety of licensing various types of pharmaceuticals (Murswieck 1992).

Although this variety of advice may exist for the taking in most industrialized countries, it is more often than not eschewed. There is a tendency for organizations to be colonized by a single perspective on the problem and therefore by a single set of experts. In unitary regimes with parliamentary governments, this may mean that only a restricted range of views may be heard on any issue. More plural regimes may permit a wider range of views to be heard. Further, some political systems such as those of Scandinavia are open to a variety of views and encourage diversity rather than restrict access. It is not clear that the policies selected in such open systems are substantially superior to those adopted in more closed systems. It is, however, clear that 'expertise' is given a much broader definition in such systems.

Are the experts accessible to decision-makers?

The third question follows closely from the second. Once we become aware of who knows what about the problem (as identified) those expert resources must be marshalled to address the problem. If the experts considered most relevant are already attached to the public organization made responsible for the problem (as they certainly should be in most cases) then there will be relatively little difficulty in using the advice. The experts may be civil servants or members of advisory structures attached to the organization, but they will be available. The use of these available experts will tend to ensure that little new advice and few new perspectives will be advanced concerning the problem, but at least there will be the comfort of having experts ready at hand.

Even if the relevant experts are not attached directly to the organizations charged with making the policy, they may still be available. This may require, however, developing new networks or dealing with some other organizations in government. If the capture of the problem has involved a political fight, then admitting that some other expertise is needed may be seen as an admission of defeat. Further, it may only institutionalize the conflicts that exist within science over the issue itself. Perhaps the most shaming outcome may be that a country has to go beyond its own scientific establishment to seek advice, or that its own policy advisers are seen to be inadequate. The competition between CERN and American physicists is one example of this possibility while the competition and conflict between American and French medical researchers over the nature and treatment of AIDS is another. In general, no organization and no country likes to admit defeat and may struggle along with inadequate advice rather than seek it externally. This may have serious consequences for the quality of the policy decisions taken.

If the decision-makers responsible for a decision with a strong element of science and technology choose to rationalize and accept their existing advice, or if they sincerely believe that this advice is 'good enough', they risk serious error. What Herbert Simon has termed a 'satisficing' strategy (receiving what may appear a reasonable minimum of advice) may be very acceptable and even very successful in some policy areas but it is unlikely to be so in policy areas involving science. While science may not be the system of accepted fact that its supporters would like to believe, still there has been progress and there are some ideas which are superior to others. Choosing to accept the *status quo* of advice too readily may harm government policy at an earlier stage of scientific development and may produce policy failures. The problem, however, is that advice and consideration of all

alternatives is expensive (in both money and time) and decision-makers lack an
objective standard about how good is 'good enough'. Especially when a decision
must be made quickly – and many must – government may choose to satisfice and
select a policy that appears 'good enough' on the grounds of readily available
advice.

What is the information to be used for?

A great deal of the scholarly literature on public policy is written from the
perspective of the decision-maker attempting to make an optimal choice about a
policy that will best serve the 'public interest'. This is an admirable ideal and one
for which many decision-makers strive. Unfortunately, however, the real world of
policy-making is not so neat as that and decisions may be made for a number of
reasons. Some, as pointed out above, may be made for the good of the organization
rather than (necessarily) for the good of society. Others may be made to simplify
a complex decision problem and to take up as little time and money as possible.
Others may be made simply because something has to be done to make a response
to a perceived difficult problem. Given the variety of goals that may be involved
in a decision, it is not surprising that information and advice might be sought for a
variety of reasons. In addition to being used for 'real' decision-making, the most
common use of advice is to legitimate a decision that an organization wanted to
make anyway.

By training and experience, many people in government positions are experts
in their policy domains. To the public, however, they may be only 'bureaucrats'
lacking the necessary ability to make difficult decisions about complex policy
areas. Therefore, these civil servants (or even ministers) may have to go through
elaborate procedures to legitimate their own decisions by citing expert advice. If
they are indeed knowledgeable about the issues, they will also know which experts
to go to for a concurrent decision; those experts will probably already be 'on tap'
for the organization. In other societies, the legitimation process may not be so
simple. If a society structures its policy-making institutions to be open to a diversity
of views, the legitimation will mean opening up the process to a number of views.
The civil servant or minister may still be able to make the decision, so long as it is
not 'arbitrary or capricious', but having conflicting expert advice on the public
record makes that decision potentially more suspect. Therefore, it is easier for
government organizations and their members if advice can be kept to more closed
and more predictable sources. Even in countries (such as Britain) that have
attempted to do that, the spread of expertise and the rise of policy communities
(Jordan and Richardson 1982 and 1987; Rhodes 1988) makes openness more likely
and more intrusive.

A perfect and dramatic example of these points arose in Britain in 1989–90
concerning BSE or 'mad cow disease' following an outbreak in some herds of beef
cattle of this previously uncommon but fatal disease of the brain and nervous
tissues. Could it be contracted by human beings, either directly by their own
beef-eating or indirectly through contact with their beef-eating dogs and cats – (one

or two cats had recently become BSE's first known feline victims)? BSE was obviously increasing. Was eating beef safe? The Ministry of Agriculture, Fisheries and Food is both the statutory guardian of food safety and the government's official sponsor of the beef-cattle industry. Its standing advisory scientific committee confirmed that science knew of no evidence that BSE could affect a human being. Some projected this fact 'positively' with practical advice: eating beef was 'perfectly safe'. Others did so with the double negative: there was no evidence that it was not safe. Herein lay the nub of a potential commercial and political crisis.

The Minister, a naturally assertive man with a propensity to preach, took up the simpler of these scientific judgments with increasing emphasis and conviction as beef sales dropped and continental European governments moved to ban their imports until tighter health checks were in place. Initial sales losses were not fully restored; the beef industry was troubled (and somewhat critical of government); the opposition parties were alleging official tardiness and even complacency. The Minister seemed genuinely bewildered – what else could he do but accept the 'best scientific advice' that the absence of incriminating evidence against BSE meant the absence of risk? Beef was, indeed, 'perfectly safe' and costly slaughtering programmes of healthy but potentially contaminated cattle were not necessary.

This was a simple case of a government taking its stand on its official scientific advice and hoping to convince both domestic and continental consumers. To base public policy on the fact that no evidence directly acquitted BSE of a human link would be absurd. The Minister seemed unwilling, therefore, to 'go beyond his advice' and take purely precautionary measures – just in case the BSE virus started to appear in people, possibly some years hence. The farmers' leaders wanted this: the Treasury, which would have paid out considerable compensation, no doubt did not.

The House of Commons agriculture committee reported in July 1990 that the Minister should see the public interest (as against the scientific) case for going beyond his advice. (It noted that he had already done so in some recent legal regulations on slaughtering on which he had told the House that they were not based on technical need but on his wish to give the consumer 'Rolls Royce protection'. However, this action had, presumably deliberately, gained almost no publicity compared with his familiar message of complete safety.) The committee recommended more such precautions. This report, with its published evidence from a further range of experts, together with earlier statements by some of the Ministry's scientific advisers and the farmers' national leader, introduced some plural debate to the official simplicity. In particular, the Ministry's chief veterinary officer chose the double negative explanations of BSE's threat and added that, of course, only complete abstinence from beef could exclude all risk from it. Interestingly, the committee urged further precautions running beyond the scientific evidence partly because it felt that the public does not entirely trust scientists. This fact (if fact it is) has probably now been added to at least one Minister's political lexicon as a result of this illuminating episode.

How is the advice to be institutionalized?

A final decision which governments must make about the advice they seek and receive about scientific and technical issues is what structures should be used. There are a number of options and most governments will use at least one for ongoing advice; most will use several. Further, if there are perceived crises, another range of options for advice may be opened and governments may spread their nets even wider to capture more advice. The modes of seeking advice will have a significant effect on the quality of the science advice received and its utility in making policies (Barker 1992a; Peters and Barker 1992).

Some institutions for advice are contained within government itself. As noted, civil servants may themselves be experts, although the degree of expertise varies markedly across countries. These experts may be concentrated within a few organizations, such as ministries of science and technology, or they may be spread more widely across the ministries that require scientific advice. Spreading the more qualified civil servants widely tends to generate conflicts over which organization and which approach is the correct one, although concentration of scientific advice in a single organization may tend to produce premature 'closure' and a single view of 'good' policy (Liberatore and Tournon, in this volume). The possibilities of conflict among organizations may be exacerbated when there are bodies in the legislature such as the Office of Technology Assessment in the United States (O'Brien and Marchand 1982; Goggin 1986; Shuyer 1989) or the House of Lords select committee on science in the United Kingdom (Williams 1992) that are also engaged in the science policy advice business. It may be, however, that no matter how it is structured, science experts that are housed within government itself will never have the legitimacy that external experts – from academe, consultancy or even industry – can command (Barker 1992b).

Advisory committees and science advisers to government are usually able to command greater legitimacy than civil servants can. Government can often get some of the best and brightest in science to participate on its committees, unless the issues involved (biological or nuclear warfare) produce some moral qualms. This allows the recommendations of the committees to carry a great deal of weight with the public and to make opposition to them less likely. Just as expert civil servants could be spread among a number of organizations or concentrated, so too can advisory committees be centralized or departmental. The latter is the more common pattern, given the wide range of specialities that could be needed if all the scientific needs of government were to be covered in a single committee. Such general committees can, however, be useful in settling questions of priorities among competing uses of scientific funds. A special case of the single central authority is the Science Adviser to government. In this case one individual, perhaps assisted by staff, is placed in the position of channelling scientific advice to government. This places a great deal of power in the hands of that one individual. Further, no matter how distinguished and broadminded the single advisers may be, they are bound to have prejudices born out of their discipline or some school within it. Thus, the advice that will come in such a setting may contain bias, whether intended or not, by the person offering the advice. The disadvantages of that bias may be offset by the ability of 'science' to speak with one voice within government and therefore to make a case for research or for a particular approach to a public problem, when that is needed.

Finally, science advice to government may be institutionalized in networks rather than in formal structures. Science advice may come by way of 'the private chat' rather than a meeting of an august committee. Such an approach has the principal virtue of encouraging the adviser's frankness. There is no need to mince words or be concerned about an unpopular opinion being made public. On the other hand, advice offered in this way does not have as great a capacity to legitimate as would other sources of scientific advice. Merely saying, 'Our experts advise ... ' does not have the weight of identifying real experts who do, in fact, advise in that way. Thus, if the advice is needed principally to legitimate decisions, then more overt forms – such as committees or formal advisers – may be desirable. But making difficult choices may be done better in a more private, informal way. A recent major example of this idea is the British Department of Education and Science declaring in early 1991 that it would henceforth receive official advice on science research spending priorities from its Advisory Board in secret. The five spending agencies (the Research Councils) and all other interested observers would no longer know (fully and officially, at least) what the Board had advised about their spending bids and policy priorities and were naturally displeased. The obvious guess is that Ministers expected their senior scientist advisers to be much tougher on some of their colleagues if they knew that their views would remain secret. Thus, as is generally the case, the design of public organizations must depend a great deal upon the purposes they are to serve and the policies which they will have to make and implement.

DEMOCRACY AND SCIENCE

This brief list of questions has demonstrated some of the problems which governments face when they must seek scientific or technical advice. This process is relatively simple if the government organization in question has a clear idea of what it wants and has close links with the experts that it wants to use. The process becomes substantially more difficult when the problem is less clearly defined, or when there are multiple and conflicting sources of advice. An organization may have to engage in overt political conflict to get its own way and 'capture' the problem and the associated resources. In short, although science implies the pure pursuit of knowledge to many people, in the public sector it also involves a political process. That process may appear to be conducted for the benefit of government itself, but by opening up the processes of science policy-making to greater scrutiny and a different set of values (political ones) the final quality of the decisions taken may actually be improved (Collingridge and Reeve 1986).

Science casts a powerful spell over many citizens, and many policy-makers, in contemporary democracies. There may be, as implied above, the need to deal with

science as an important, but not unchallenged, source of advice for policy. This
challenging will arise through the processes of representative democracy and
organizational politics in almost all countries. In others, mechanisms for involving
social groups in policy-making or even mechanisms of direct democracy (referenda
on nuclear power in Sweden, Italy and Austria) may present even greater challenges
to the dominance of science. There are at least three reasons for the consideration
of a much greater public role in science policy in contemporary industrialized
democracies.

Firstly, society has certain persistent needs which may or may not fit with the
current fashions in science. Many citizens may prefer a crash programme to find
cheap, non-polluting energy sources rather than send a huge telescope into outer
space. Others may prefer a programme to solve problems of recycling plastics
rather than get another particle accelerator. The more mundane projects may not
excite many scientists and it might be difficult to mobilize resources for those
programmes, but they are clearly pressing social needs. There must be some means
of balancing those needs against the fashions of science and the desires of scientists
to pursue their own programmes of research. That means is usually government.

Following from the above, there must be some balancing of the needs of
academic producers of knowledge and the consumers. This to some degree may be
a balance between science and technology, but the issue may go even deeper than
that. The determination of what is important to address through science and of what
knowledge is needed for society tends to be dominated by the producers. This is
analogous to many other policy areas where producer interests dominate over
clients or consumers. In the case of scientific research, however, the ability of
consumers to influence policy may be even more restricted. The clients of social
service agencies, even if they are of lower socio-economic status, can say what
they need and how they are living. The 'clients' of scientific research funded
through the public sector may not even be able to articulate what they want, or what
the options are. This disabled stance as client can apply even to governments
themselves. This absence of knowledge may well exclude them from effective
participation. This, in turn, means that some system of proxy advocacy may be
required for effective consumer representations in science policy. Openness of
advice systems has functioned somewhat in this manner, but options for in-
stitutionalizing informed public intervention may be of value.

The final and related concern is the circular and close connection between public
policy and science. To some extent the progress of science may motivate policy,
either to take advantage of the possibilities opened by new discoveries, or to attempt
to correct for the difficulties created by those discoveries. On the other hand, policy
may motivate scientific change and political demands for certain types of advancement (such as 'wars on cancer') may generate scientific change. The danger is
that good policy may not generate very good science (Rushefsky 1986) just as good
science may not always produce good policy. So this requires that policy-makers
and scientists understand the limits of science, as well as the limits of the ability of
policies to create new (and perhaps desperately needed) knowledge. Government

and science policy cannot afford to exist in isolation from each other, but must find ways to accommodate their different cultures and differing needs.

Barker, A. (1992a), Patterns of decision advice processing: a review of types and a commentary on some recent British practices; in Peters, B.G. and Barker, A. (eds) (1992) *op. cit.*

Barker, A. (1992b), Professionalised expertise and the politics of British land-use planning; in Peters, B.G. and Barker, A. (eds), *op. cit.*

Collingridge, D. and Reeve, C. (1986), *Science Speaks to Power: The role of experts in policy-making* (London: Pinter).

Douglas, M. (1985), *Risk Acceptability According to the Social Sciences* (New York: Russell Sage).

Douglas, M. and Wildavsky, A. (1982), *Risk and Culture* (Berkeley, CA: University of California Press).

Downs, A. (1967), *Inside Bureaucracy* (Boston, MA: Little, Brown).

Dror, Y. (1983), Policy-gambling: a preliminary exploration; *Policy Studies Journal,* 12, 9–13.

Dunn, W.N. (1981), *Public Policy Analysis* (Englewood Cliffs, NJ: Prentice-Hall).

Fischer, F. (1990), *Technocracy and the Politics of Expertise* (Newbury Park, CA: Sage).

Goggin, M. (1986), *Governing Science and Technology in a Democracy* (Knoxville, TN: University of Tennessee Press).

Grove, J.W. (1989), *In Defense of Science: Science, technology and politics in modern society* (Toronto: University of Toronto Press).

Howson, C. and Urbach, P. (1989), *Scientific Reasoning: A Bayesian approach* (LaSalle, IL: Open Court Press).

Jordan, A.G. and Richardson, J.J. (1982), The British policy style or the logic of negotiation; in Richardson, J.J. (ed.) (1982), *Policy Styles in Western Europe* (London: Allen & Unwin).

Jordan, A.G. and Richardson, J.J. (1987), *Government and Pressure Groups in Britain* (New York: Oxford University Press).

Kuhn, T.S.C. (1962), *The Structure of Scientific Revolutions* (Chicago, IL: Chicago University Press).

Murswieck, A. (1992), Policy advice and decision-making in the German federal bureaucracy; in Peters, B.G. and Barker, A. (eds), *op. cit.*

O'Brien, D.M. and Marchand, D.A. (1982), *The Politics of Technology Assessment: Institutions, processes and political disputes* (Lexington, MA: Lexington Books).

O'Riordan, T., Kemp, R. and Purdue, M. (1988), *Sizewell B: An anatomy of the inquiry* (London: Macmillan).

Peters, B.G. and Barker, A. (eds) (1992), *Advising West European Governments: Inquiries, expertise and public policy* (Edinburgh: Edinburgh University Press).

Rhodes, R. (1988), *Beyond Westminster and Whitehall: The sub-central governments of Britain* (London: Unwin Hyman).

Rubenstein, M.F. (1975), *Patterns of Problem Solving* (Englewood Cliffs, NJ: Prentice-Hall).

Rushefsky, M.E. (1986), *Making Cancer Policy* (Albany, NY: State University of New York Press).

Schneider, J.W. (1985), Social problems theory: the constructivist view; *American Review of Sociology,* 11, 209–29.

Shuyer, S. (1989), How to Revolutionize Washington with 140 people; *Washington Monthly,* 21, (June) 38–41 .

Singer, O. (1992), Knowledge and politics in economic policy-making: economic advisers in USA, Britain and West Germany in the post-Keynesian period; in Peters, B.G. and Barker, A. (eds), *op. cit.*

Street, J. (1992), Policy advice in an established official advice structure: AIDS advice through the British Department of Health; in Peters, B.G. and Barker, A. (eds), *op. cit.*

Weinberg, A.M. (1972a), Science and trans-science; *Minerva*, 10, 209–22.

Weinberg, A.M. (1972b), Social institutions and nuclear energy; *Science*, 177, 27–34.

Williams, R. (1992), The House of Lords Select Committee on Science and Technology within British science policy and the nature of science policy advice; in Peters, B.G. and Barker, A. (eds), *op. cit.*

Two

Sources of Technological Controversy
Proximity To or Alienation From Technology?

WOLFGANG RÜDIG

This chapter looks behind both the formal and informal processes of
scientific advice-giving to public policy-makers. It asks how the
divisions of opinion, or even of 'philosophy', concerning major technological subjects such as nuclear power arise, particularly among the
scientific practitioners or administrators and other experts themselves.
The sources of this dissent among experts may be traced to both their
personal proximity to and their alienation from the core of the controversial technology in question – as notably in the example outlined here of
nuclear power. However, the findings have wide-ranging implications
for the assessment of technology in general.

INTRODUCTION

Technological developments have in recent years attracted increasing criticism,
rejection and public protest. Nuclear technologies have been among the most
prominent subjects of such adverse reactions.

The emergence of political controversy and public debate over major technological developments brought a new political role to scientists and technologists.
They were certainly no strangers to political controversy *per se* . But previously,
such conflicts had mostly been conducted outside the glare of publicity and public
interest, contained within the confines of individual policy sectors. Controversies
over nuclear safety brought scientists and technologists into the centre of a major
political conflict about the development of a particular technology.

Overwhelmingly, scientists and technologists have appeared as promoters of
particular technologies, defending them against what they often see as 'emotional',
scientifically uninformed resistance. But also, scientists have emerged as important
critics of technology, expressing dissent in the public domain and lending their

support to protest movements opposing particular technological developments. Certainly, dissent among scientists and technologists about particular technologies is likely to have a broader public impact only if it corresponds with existing sensibilities in the mass media and among the general public. On the other hand, protest against technologies is unlikely to gain much legitimacy if it cannot register the support of some recognized expert opinion (Nelkin 1975; Nowotny 1977; Conrad 1982).

This new role of scientists raises a number of questions about the sources of such technological controversies. Do scientists play a role in subverting the progress of particular technologies or do they legitimize it? Does their proximity to technology encourage contempt or devotion?

This apparently contradictory role of science in technological controversies will be analysed in this paper. First, we will look at two different approaches to explain the source of technological controversy with concepts of proximity and alienation from technology. The value of these approaches is then tested in a case study about controversies regarding the safety of nuclear technologies. The discussion of the case study material will then lead to some general hypotheses on the role of proximity to technology and its subverting and legitimizing functions.

SOURCES OF EXPERT DISSENT

In the popular conception of science, the idea of a 'scientific controversy' is rather alien. Science as the provider of recognized 'truth' leaves little room for the idea that 'scientists' could persistently disagree over a matter recognized as amenable to scientific enquiry. Scientists may disagree about matters of public policy, perhaps, but not on the essential 'facts' which are supposed to guide it.

Such a simplistic view of science was long ago dismantled by the sociology of science. The social negotiation not only of the process of scientific research but also scientific knowledge as such has been demonstrated by a number of works (Barnes and Edge 1982; Knorr-Cetina and Mulkay 1983; Collins 1982, 1985; Latour and Woolgar 1986; Latour 1987).

A first conception of scientific controversies can be derived from Kuhn's (1962) famous analysis of scientific paradigms. The most profound and persistent disagreements among scientists can be seen as the result of paradigmatic discrepancies. This highest degree of scientific controversy differs from others in that there appears to be no theoretical construction, experiment, or data-gathering process which can provide a resolution to the controversy one way or the other.

But also within accepted paradigms, controversy within science cannot be seen as the exception. Rather, science itself can be defined as a process of continued controversy over, say, the adequacy of experiments, data and theories. In this sense, controversy is endemic to science. Only at the end of the scientific process do we have what sociologists of science call a 'closure' of scientific controversies – which is identical with the end of the conduct of 'science' in terms of data collection, experiments, and conclusions drawn.

From the vantage point of the sociology of science, controversy is thus not some exceptional phenomenon but an intrinsic element of the scientific process. This contrasts with the demands made on science in terms of public policy and decision-making. Science is put in a difficult, even an impossible, position to provide 'truth' if all it can actually provide are hypotheses of different degrees of acceptability.

As a result, science has a double function. It can legitimate with expert consensus after 'closure'. But the scientific process also implies a critical if 'subversive' attitude, potentially undermining the first function. With the increasing industrialization of science and the growing demand, in return, of science serving as a source of legitimation for the development and dissemination of potentially controversial technologies, the scientific process could thus be expected to act as a source of scepticism undermining the certainty of knowledge about technology and its effects.

This is the essential background to Collins' thesis that 'certainty about natural phenomena ... tends to vary inversely with proximity to the scientific work' (Collins 1986 2). Collins elaborates further in a later article:

> Close proximity to experimental work, particularly where there is an element of controversy, makes visible the skilful, inexplicable and therefore potentially fallible aspects of experimentation ... Thus, there is more certainty when distance from the cutting edge of science is maximized ... distance from the cutting edge of science is the source of what certainty we have. (Collins 1988 726)

Scientific dissent about technological development, we may thus presume, is most likely to occur where the 'experiment' is still both the crucial experience and also the indicator of the 'proximity' of the scientists to a technology.

Such a theory of scientific controversies, one might argue, could have only very limited applications in the realm of technological politics. Perhaps it may even be based on a view of science which is obsolete in view of the progressive industrialization and militarization of science. In particular, one has to wonder what role the adherence to the uncertainties of experimental science can play if an apparently overwhelming majority of scientists and engineers predominantly appear in the function of defending technological developments in the face of public scepticism. Uncertainty and scepticism, one might even argue, lie more with the scientifically illiterate whose 'gut' rejection of 'big technology' appears more vindicated in the wake of major technological disasters (Bhopal, Challenger, Chernobyl) than the increasingly vain attempts at reassurance emanating from the 'scientific' authorities.

A rival theory focuses more strongly on the degree of alienation from science and technology as a main source of dissent and controversy. A number of studies have shown that members and supporters of protest movements against nuclear technology are generally employed in the non-industrial service sector, such as education and the arts, or stand outside the formal economy altogether (Lowe and Rüdig 1986). In other words, they are removed from the centres of scientific and technological development and have no 'inside' experience or knowledge of it. Their alienation from 'high-tech' appears thus not to be a result of a high level of acquired knowledge of technology.

This also seems to be broadly true of dissenting scientists in the case of nuclear power. It appears that scientists lending their support to the critics of nuclear energy come predominantly from scientific disciplines which are further removed from 'industrialized' science than others. Nowotny (1979) finds in her study of the nuclear debate in Austria that scientists critical of nuclear energy have predominantly had 'unorthodox', less structured, careers outside the main scientific-industrial laboratories. They were also more likely to come from the biological, medical and social sciences than from physics or chemistry. Pro-nuclear scientists had predominantly 'straight' and highly structured careers.

On another level, we could postulate that it is alienation rather than proximity which stimulates dissent: in the case of controversies over nuclear reactor choices, the lack of knowledge and high uncertainty over foreign reactor designs provided a major stumbling-block for their adoption in countries such as Britain, Canada, and France which had developed their own reactor technology (Rüdig 1988). Alienation from a particular technological design, say the American light water reactors, could thus be associated with proximity to and high certainty concerning a rival design, such as Britain's advanced gas-cooled reactor. Again, we would have a case here where proximity to one design leads to a strong attachment to it accompanied by alienation from and rejection of alternative designs.

In the analysis of technological controversies, we are thus faced with two apparently contradictory approaches, focusing respectively on proximity to and alienation from a technology as sources of controversy. As we shall see, these concepts are perhaps not as far removed from each other as may appear. Both concepts, of proximity and alienation, require some further clarification, which the following case study may assist.

CONTROVERSY OVER NUCLEAR TECHNOLOGY: A CASE STUDY

Nuclear technologies have been the subject of a variety of scientific and other controversies. The controversy of the effect of the fall-out from nuclear weapons testing in the 1950s and 1960s was the first major controversy (Kopp 1979; Divine 1978). It spilled over into the nuclear energy field by providing the major input into the controversy over the effects of routine emissions of radioactivity from nuclear power stations (Sternglass 1973; Gofman and Tamplin 1971; Nowotny and Hirsch 1980; Mazur 1981). Another major issue has concerned nuclear waste disposal (Fallows 1979).

For this section one controversy of nuclear technology is selected because it is particularly well documented and was in many ways the crucial controversy which provided the starting-point for the formation of an organized national anti-nuclear campaign in the United States: the controversy about emergency core cooling systems.

The debate over the adequacy of these systems became a major public issue in the United States in the early 1970s. The background to the debate was the rapid commercialization of nuclear reactors which had taken place in the 1960s. Two reactor manufacturers, Westinghouse and General Electric, had achieved a commercial breakthrough on the US market. After selling cheap 'loss-leader' reactors to establish themselves on the market, both companies had convinced electricity utilities in the United States that the economies of scale which could be achieved with the construction of large nuclear power stations made nuclear energy competitive with fossil-fuel power stations.

One problem of this development was that neither reactor manufacturers nor utilities had any experience in the construction and operation of such large nuclear reactors. On the one hand, this led to construction delays and large cost overruns with substantial financial losses (Perry *et al.* 1977; Bupp and Derian 1978). But, also, it confronted the regulatory agency, the Atomic Energy Commission (AEC) with new safety problems.

The much larger size of the light water reactors (LWRs) built in the 1960s created various problems. It was feared that the much bigger cores would overheat and melt more easily and that containment would not be sufficient to hold the large amounts of radioactivity which would be released in such a case. In these terms, the LWR had a lower 'intrinsic' safety than other reactor designs. The LWR's power density (the heat released by the core per unit volume) is much higher, posing a higher risk of overheating. While in other reactors a loss of coolant would leave the moderator (graphite or heavy water) as a heat sink, slowing down the temperature rise, the LWR uses light water as both its moderator and coolant in one system. Its loss would therefore leave no other substance to absorb the excess heat (Patterson 1976 80–3).

To counteract this particular danger of the LWR, a safety device was called for which could provide cooling of the core in an emergency. The problem was that at the time of the commercial breakthrough of LWR technology in the 1960s, the technology of emergency core cooling systems was still largely unproven. The AEC had thus to contend with enormous uncertainties. From the beginning, the AEC had never had the resources and expertise to evaluate applications independently of the parties who had an interest in them. Increasingly, the AEC became dependent on the information provided by the utilities and manufacturers themselves. Safety assessment was largely subservient to the dominant AEC and industrial interests in accelerated nuclear development. This was essentially also the policy pursued with regard to the 1960s construction boom (Rolph 1979).

This time, however, dissent within the AEC grew stronger than before. It first came mainly from the Advisory Committee on Reactor Safeguards (ACRS), a body intended to present independent scientific advice to the AEC. The ACRS was extremely worried about the siting of large reactors with unproven technologies close to major population centres. The AEC put pressure on the ACRS not to publicize its view but to express any reservations only in private. The ACRS complied, not wanting to jeopardize the commercial development of nuclear technology. But the AEC moved only very slowly on LWR safety. Its main research effort had been tied up with the liquefied metal fast breeder reactor.

Following pressure from the ACRS, the AEC commissioned in October 1966 a report on meltdown accidents, an edited version of which was published a year later as the Ergen Report. It expressed some minor reservations and asked for further research. Safety research on LWRs was eventually stepped up, with more attention now being paid to the emergency core cooling system problem. A series of experiments was commissioned with models of these systems to be carried out at the Reactor Testing Station in Idaho (Rolph 1979; Ford 1984).

In 1967 the Ergen Report had not attracted much attention. The increasing general salience of environmental issues the proliferation of local conflict over nuclear installations (Nelkin 1971; Lewis 1973) and the widely publicized dissent of two AEC scientists, Drs Gofman and Tamplin, in 1969 over the effect of low level radiation emanating from nuclear power stations (Nowotny and Hirsch 1980; Mazur 1981) had all attracted public attention. In addition to internal pressure from the ACRS, the AEC had thus increasingly to contend with public mistrust of nuclear technology.

A number of experiments with emergency core cooling system devices were carried out by engineers at the Idaho Reactor Testing Station. Particularly significant were six tests undertaken with a 'tea-kettle-size' model of a pressurized water reactor (PWR) in the winter of 1970–1. The ECCS did not quite function as planned. Simulating a loss-of-coolant accident caused by a major pipe rupture, the Idaho engineers found that the ECCS would release additional cooling water but that it would bypass the core and escape out of the same hole as the normal cooling water. A special report documenting these test results, the Brockett Report, was completed in April 1971.

The results, which were known in January of 1971, startled the AEC. The American nuclear industry was in the middle of a gigantic construction effort with more than fifty reactors under construction at the time. The AEC decided to set up a special task force, the Hanauer Task Force, to look into the matter.

The crucial issue which presented itself to the task force was whether the 'tea-kettle-size' experiments of ECCS behaviour or computer modelling of ECCS behaviour in a meltdown accident were more reliable guides. The nuclear construction industry had based all its plans and formal construction applications on such computer models. They argued that the Idaho experiments were too unlike the situation of a real meltdown accident to be of any value for regulatory policy. The Idaho team, on the other hand, disputed the value of these computer models as they were based on a number of arbitrary assumptions. Their experiments had led to results which were incompatible with the computer predictions. No one really knew what would go on inside a nuclear reactor in a meltdown accident and it was beyond existing technology and scientific knowledge to find out.

The AEC commissioned another series of experiments, this time involving the reactor industry itself. But their results were unacceptable to the Idaho scientists who severely criticized the way they were conducted. Other AEC scientists joined in the criticism. The Hanauer Task Force was, however, unimpressed by this dissent. It declared in June 1971 that the reactor industry's computer models were sufficient to approve current ECCS designs and to license nuclear power stations on that basis.

The AEC's handling of the ECCS issue alienated many of its own scientists who had been involved in experimental work on nuclear safety. That dissent at first remained purely internal. Rumours of the results of the Idaho tea-kettle tests had, however, leaked out, and were finally made public knowledge in May 1971. The issue had come to the attention of a group of scientists outside the industry who were working for the Cambridge, Massachusetts-based Union of Concerned Scientists (UCS). The UCS had begun to take an interest in civil nuclear energy following plans to construct a nuclear power station in the region at Plymouth. Following up on available information, UCS scientists had no difficulty finding AEC scientists eager to speak out. In particular, scientists at the AEC's Oak Ridge Laboratories – where a series of experiments on the behaviour of fuel rods in a loss-of-coolant accident also had shown worrying results, only to be abandoned by the AEC in February 1971 – made no secret to MIT Physics Professor Howard Kendall (who was leading the UCS investigation) that they and a sizeable number of colleagues at other AEC laboratories were seriously worried about the ECCS question.

The ECCS issue was now raised at a number of formal public licensing hearings concerning new nuclear power stations and this threatened to cause major delays. The AEC decided to settle the issue once and for all with a policy-making ('rule-making') public hearing, after which the matter could not be raised in individual licensing hearings.

That strategy backfired badly and developed into a public relations disaster for the AEC. The UCS and other groups were not only able (with the help of the Freedom of Information Act) to extract documents incriminating the AEC but also dissenting AEC scientists volunteered to supply the objectors with a wealth of inside documents and other information. In addition, several AEC scientists gave public evidence expressing their reservation about the AEC's handling of LWR safety.

The hearing, originally planned to last six weeks, took two years – from January 1972 to December 1973 – to complete. It established that senior AEC scientists had major reservations about key safety aspects of nuclear power. This was, incidentally, not enough to shift the AEC's determination to pursue its chosen course. At the end of the hearing its position was still that computer models of ECCS behaviour were adequate and that no pause in licensing could be justified on these grounds (Ford 1984 85–130; Primack and Hippel 1974 208–235).

What are the key points arising from this case for the purpose of our investigation? First, dissent was based on the testing of model equipment, on experimental work on the operationalizability of a technical device. We can observe two sides of the conflict which are equally 'close' to the technology, but whose relation to it has a different basis: those 'testing' a technology were confronted by those whose primary interest was to disseminate the technology.

Second, the substantial issue at hand does not, at first sight, differ significantly from scientific controversies: the adequacy of experimental designs, data and theoretical models was in question. However, two special circumstances moved this controversy away from a model of scientific controversies: the stakes involved, and the question of the adequacy of 'scientific' methods as such.

The stakes involved were substantial: the reactor construction industry had made a first breakthrough in the early 1960s, but high cost-overruns threatened the boom of nuclear construction and it collapsed in the late 1960s. As Bupp and Derian (1978) argue, the nuclear market might have remained collapsed in the early 1970s but for the rise in fossil fuel prices and uncertainty over future oil prices and availability which in fact provided the grounds for a second construction boom.

The ECCS debate threatened that second boom. The demands of scientists for further, more detailed experimental work implicitly challenged AEC policy not to delay the licensing of nuclear reactors as applications poured in in the early 1970s. As throughout its previous history, the AEC's function as the promoter of nuclear technology took precedence over its role as regulator. Countless occasions can be cited in which doubts about particular safety aspects were couched in the conditional mode: a solution to such problems had to be found which did not jeopardize the continued licensing of nuclear reactors. The question of a temporary moratorium of licensing was thought to be out of the question as it was feared that the industry's momentum could be lost, perhaps for ever. (The Commission retained its dual, promoter-regulator, function until 1978, when it was divided into a promotional agency and the new Nuclear Regulatory Commission.)

In terms of the substance of the controversy, it must be doubted if even a far more detailed research programmeme on LWR safety at that stage would have settled the issue and 'closed' the controversy. The dissent of AEC scientists and their readiness to bring it into the public domain was certainly a result of what appears to have been a rather insensitive handling of the issue by the AEC. A more responsive AEC may have been more successful in avoiding the alienation of its own scientists. But, on a more fundamental note, the nature of the technology involved makes it extremely difficult to 'close' the controversy: computer models as well as model experiments can provide only more or less adequate approximations of a situation which it is impossible to simulate under full operational conditions. It is that aspect which limits the possibility of 'closure' once doubts on the technology have emerged.

The brief case study we have presented here confirms the presence of two forms of expert dissent on technology: critical sentiment towards nuclear technology may have its roots in remoteness from the technology as well as in close proximity to it.

Does familiarity with a technology thus breed contempt or devotion? The solution to this analytical dilemma, we would argue, lies in a closer definition of the relation to a technology. What exactly is the basis on which 'experiences' with nuclear technology are received? To start with, the findings of the ECCS case study confirm the hypothesis on the 'subversive' role of the experiment. It was those scientists concerned with an experimental relation to nuclear technology (the Idaho experiments with model ECCS systems) whose confidence in the operational use of both technologies was lowest and who were one important source of scientific dissent.

However, in assessing the role of the experiment in this context, one has to reflect on the rather special character of those experiments in the context of the development of nuclear technology. Those special conditions make it rather doubtful, we would suggest, whether the making of experiments can fulfil such a function as a potential source of scientific uncertainty in the case of all new technologies.

What is so special about the experiments described in our case study? The important point is that a trial and error research, development and dissemination process which has been followed for most other technologies so far cannot fully apply to nuclear technology. This has been particularly obvious in the case of nuclear power reactors. And this is not a point which is made only by those critical of nuclear power.

In particular, Alvin Weinberg, a nuclear design engineer who was involved in pioneering work from the early days of nuclear development, and Wolf Häfele, a German nuclear scientist mainly known for his work on the fast breeder reactor, have put forward a startling theory of technological development which in particular focuses on the necessary exclusion of the experiment and the scientific process.

According to Weinberg and Häfele, the nature of nuclear development makes the trial and error path impossible. This is so essentially either because the consequences of error are far too great (a major reactor accident) or the time-scale involved for the proper evaluation of its impact is prohibitively long (the health effect of low level radiation and the implications of the long-term storage of highly active nuclear waste) (Weinberg 1972a; Häfele 1974). Such an observation might well serve to instil scepticism as to the wisdom of proceeding on the nuclear road. This is recognized but instantly dismissed:

> If properly interpreted and understood, the public concern about nuclear power is not unfounded. But that concern is not a simple function of a peculiarity of nuclear power. It is, rather, the general condition of civilization towards which we are moving; it is a condition where the magnitude of human enterprises becomes comparable with the magnitude of the widest determinants of our normal existence. Nuclear power turns out to be a forerunner, a pathfinder, of that. (Häfele 1974 317)

Häfele thus effectively predicts a new era of industrialization which makes redundant the traditional scepticism and trial and error of the scientific process. Taking the place of science in this scenario is what Weinberg calls 'trans-science' which serves as an ideology to the 'new priesthood' of nuclear scientists which has to be formed to provide the social basis for the longevity of social institutions which the use of nuclear energy entails (Weinberg 1972b).

The 'trans-scientific' character of nuclear technology must be seen as the major source of expert dissent in this area. Nuclear power technology cannot be defaulted on an experimental basis. Any experiments conducted on, say, the adequacy of nuclear reactor safety features can try to approach, but can never achieve, full operational conditions. From what Weinberg and Häfele are saying, nuclear energy could be defaulted only on the level of rejecting the logic of 'trans-science' itself. If Häfele is right that nuclear technology is only a 'pathfinder' technology for a new area of technological developments with similar characteristics, it would appear that dissent would be equivalent to a more fundamental critique of technological and industrial development as a whole. Such a link explicitly addressed by Häfele and Weinberg becomes particularly pervasive in terms of the growth and complexity of large technological systems. While individual elements and devices of such technological systems may be tested to a satisfactory degree, increasing scale and complexity make it impossible to test the full operation and impact of such systems.

Indeed, some of the anti-nuclear criticism is built on the rejection of the dynamic of industrialism as such. What Häfele and Weinberg define as a pathfinder technology is characterised by Ullrich (1979) as a 'cul-de-sac technology', using much the same criteria. A cul-de-sac technology is a technology whose environmental and social impact is incalculable and which cannot be tamed, with its destructive features removed, by submitting it to democratic control. While Weinberg and Häfele legitimate the use of nuclear power as a 'pathfinder' technology which is the only possible course for industrial society, Ullrich comes to reject the entire industrialization process, having considered the more general application of the logic of nuclear technology.

Other authors assessing the problem of nuclear power from different perspectives address the same characteristics of this technology. Charles Perrow (1984) argues that the nature of high-risk technologies, including their safety systems, is so complex that their complete control is impossible. Due to this complexity of the technological system and the 'tight-coupling' of its individual elements, any failure of individual components can have unpredictable consequences affecting the entire system. Accidents can be reduced but never totally avoided; improvements in safety measures only add to the unmanageable complexity. Accidents are thus 'normal' features of these systems. If any such accident has catastrophic and unacceptable consequences, then the only way to avoid them is to abandon such highly complex and tightly-coupled technical systems.

A similar point about the evaluation of complex technology can be made on the grounds of economic decision-making. The introduction of large technological systems largely pre-empts any independent economic analysis by creating a momentum of its own: this includes an economic framework for its continued positive evaluation. To guard against this fallacy, Collingridge has argued for dis-investment from any technological systems which evade the possibility of a continual, incremental economic evaluation (Collingridge 1983): a concept which can easily be transferred to the realm of safety risks and environmental impact.

We can now conceive of another type of source of expert dissent going beyond that based on the experiment as the source of uncertainty (as put forward by Collins). This is the dissent over the admissibility of the abandonment of the trial-and-error path of the development and dissemination of technology. Essentially, we have now reached a point where the development rationales of science and technology diverge.

At this stage, the concepts of proximity and alienation have to be reworked. The rejection of the 'trans-science' approach in favour of a maintenance of trial-and-error (and thus the implicit rejection of any technology which can not be evaluated on a trial-and-error basis) can be seen as both an expression of proximity to the scientific process and as alienation from technological development. If technological development does indeed, as Weinberg and Häfele put it, reach such a size that its impacts are by definition beyond human understanding and thus incalculable, then the continued attachment to the experiment (and, by implication, to the piecemeal, incremental, trial-and-error evaluation of such technological development) would render 'proximity to science' and 'alienation from technology' synonymous.

'Proximity to science' in this context exclusively refers to the scientific process rather than the practice of institutionalized, industrialized science. Indeed, resistance to the trans-science rationale of technological development may arise less in some scientific disciplines than others. Experimental physicists may be more aware of the limitations on experiments which can be carried out. And biologists and medical scientists may be more aware of the limitations in terms of time and number in the observation of effects of particular technologies. On a more general level, however, the identification of the 'pathfinder' paradigm with the dynamic of industrialism may make it less attractive among those scientific disciplines which have so far been least touched by the industrialization of science, such as parts of the biological sciences and, indeed, the social sciences.

So far, we have concentrated on the sources of expert dissent on nuclear energy technology. But to what extent can it be argued that our findings could be generalized to cover technology as a whole?

Nuclear energy technology is not the only technological system which is unsuited to a trial-and-error evaluation. Many areas of nuclear weapons technology, for example, also fall into this category. For example, the accuracy of nuclear missiles can never be tested under full operational conditions. In a case study of a controversy on the accuracy of nuclear missiles, MacKenzie, Rüdig and Spinardi (1988) show that there is a relation between the degree of experts' uncertainty over nuclear missile accuracy and the kind of proximity these experts have to the technology. Those engaged in attempts to carry out experiments coming as close as possible to operational conditions have a high awareness of the uncertainties involved in the assessment of missile accuracies. Least uncertainty is shown by those concerned with missile technology in administrative functions, such as military decision-makers attached to particular missile programs. Uncertainty is high again among those alienated from missile technology, for example representatives of military organizations competing with missile programs for funds and recognition.

Not all technologies, however, are like this. It is true, as the 'new sociology of technology' tries to show, that all technological developments involve elements of social negotiation and are thus socially shaped (MacKenzie and Wajcman 1985; Bijker *et al.* 1987). But we would argue that a distinction has to be made between 'cul-de-sac' technologies and other technologies.

Are the problems of technological controversy limited to technologies whose size, complexity and potential impact make a trial-and-error evaluation in principle impossible? How can we conceive of expert dissent about technology on lower levels of generality, below the distinction between 'pathfinder' and trial-and-error logics of technological development?

One can conceive of a hierarchy of technologies according to their degree of complexity, size and integration in the wider technological systems which link different technologies with each other. The 'cul-de-sac' technologies are at the top of such a hierarchy, characterized by a theoretical impossibility of full testing under operational conditions. Other complex technologies may be open to trial-and-error evaluation but only at a very high cost. In the nuclear case, for example, a case could be made that the light water reactor technology was disseminated too quickly without more adequate technical experience because of the reactor industry's desire to enter the market as quickly as possible (Bupp and Derian 1978). A comparable argument may be made for large-scale and highly complex technological apparatuses such as the US Space Shuttle. In cases of both a high cost of testing and the impossibility of testing in full operational conditions, dissent from those close to the technology could thus be expected, complaining of the inadequacy of the experiments and testing carried out.

Another well-known aspect of expert dissent which is related to size and complexity concerns the accessibility of expert knowledge. 'Simple' technologies which are easily tested are less likely to lead to dissent on their technological features, operationalizability and impact because their independent evaluation by regulatory agencies, competitors and other parties is not costly. Such evaluation is less easy with the increasing size and complexity of new technological developments, reaching a situation where only those directly involved in the development process are able to provide an evaluation of the technology. At the same time, it is this group which usually has the strongest self-interest in the further development of such technologies. In this case, familiarity with technology is the source of both dissent and support: familiarity with one device usually goes hand in hand with unfamiliarity with the rival device. Dissent is thus based on both familiarity and ignorance alike.

So far, we have mainly concerned ourselves with size and complexity. However, many technologies of various sizes are developed and used only as part of a larger technological system. Even if such a small, simple technical device can be tested on a trial-and-error basis on its own, this may cease to be so once this device is integrated into a large technological system.

Nuclear energy is thus, in our view, not an isolated case. With the profusion of other large technological systems in general, the move towards a new magnitude of human enterprise is under way despite the possible demise of nuclear energy as an important element of our technological future. Consequently, an era of uncertainty where the effect of individual actions is increasingly incalculable and where 'trans-scientific' rules apply may be already upon us.

CONCLUSIONS

Technological controversy has been seen to be identified with three sources. Firstly, there is the subversive character of the scientific process in which controversy, in a broad sense, is endemic. Closeness to that scientific process during the evaluation of technologies is thus likely to be a cause of the subverting of certainty about the features of individual technologies. Secondly, we have identified in nuclear technologies a specific class of technology notable for the intrinsic impossibility of testing under full operational conditions. The dissemination of nuclear technologies thus tends to imply a different paradigm, that of a 'trans-scientific' or 'pathfinder' role, from most other technologies which can still proceed on a trial-and-error basis of development. (This new paradigm is to be distinguished from cases where insufficient testing is the source of dissent due to the high cost of such testing in conjunction with other economic or political pressures.) Finally, there is a third level of dissent in terms of the rivalry between individual technologies, provided that their level of complexity makes it difficult to evaluate them easily from the outside. In these cases, expert dissent is based on the experts' familiarity with one technology in harness with their unfamiliarity with rival technologies.

What are the sources of loyalty and devotion to technology in the face of dissent from those particularly close to a technology as well as those alienated from it? There is evidence to suggest that proximity to technology by users, administrators and technological host communities leads to highly positive attitudes and often uncritical attachments to technology. People regularly exposed to high probability – low impact risks whose occurrence can be easily measured tend to underestimate the chance of accidents or failures. Familiarity with a technology on an everyday basis breeds 'over-confidence' (Fischhoff *et al.* 1981). There are other, related results: host communities of nuclear power stations have overwhelmingly positive attitudes to 'their' nuclear plant and are less likely to oppose further additional plants on the same site (Rüdig 1990 1991). Nuclear personnel at power stations have been found to harbour deep anxieties which have continually to be suppressed (Sivadon and Fernandez 1968; Guedeney and Mendel 1973).

In terms of certainties and uncertainties, certainty is often preserved as a protective measure to comply with the current situation of the technology user or host. In some cases, devoted technological attachments could be explained as a simple function of organizational self-interest. If the organizational purpose is to promote a particular technology, then its members are likely to develop a close identification with that purpose and to maintain it by adopting selective perceptions of the environment which fit that purpose, suppressing any uncertainties which might be associated with the technologies.

What is the relevance of these findings for the politics of scientific advice? While the advance of nuclear energy technologies has been stopped, we are still moving rapidly towards the adoption of larger and more complex technological systems in a number of other areas. Perhaps more important, just the sheer volume (rather than the quality) of industrial activities appears to bear the possibility of disastrous consequences on a global scale. The greenhouse effect, the hole in the ozone layer and acid rain are all cases which have demonstrated the essential unpredictability of the effects of using modern technology.

Unfortunately, technological decisions are frequently made or strongly influenced (if not determined) by those with attachments to technologies who find it difficult to reflect on the vagaries and social negotiation of the 'facts' they are explicitly based on. A misplaced perception of high certainty or, in other words, over-confidence may well have been the source of some recent technological disasters. Further over-confidence may have disastrous consequences on a wider scale.

Forms have to be sought to stop and correct such over-confidence. The social researcher of technology may make some contribution to this by progressing to the very heart of technology and gaining access to the uncertainties of those at the centre of technological developments (MacKenzie *et al.* 1988). The policy sciences, in particular, have to take up these issues. Social-scientific reflections on the sources of technical expertise have mainly been limited to the 'ghetto' of the sociology of sciences and have not been picked up by public policy analysts. Technology policy analysts have to penetrate the 'black box' of technological development and take account of the 'social shaping' of technology (Rüdig 1989).

The policy-maker requiring advice can guard against over-confidence only by spreading the sources of his advice and including in particular those at the 'cutting edge' of science who are able and willing to impart to policy-makers the uncertainties involved. Ultimately, the rise in the general level of uncertainty about the impact of technology at world level makes a preventative policy of removing potential sources of catastrophic development the only option.

Barnes, B. and Edge, D. (eds) (1982), *Science in Context: Readings in the sociology of science* (Milton Keynes: Open University Press).

Bijker, W.E., Hughes, T.P. and Pinch, T.J. (eds) (1987), *The Social Construction of Technological Systems: New directions in the sociology and history of technology* (Cambridge, MA: MIT Press).

Bupp, I.C. and Derian, J. C. (1978), *Light Water: How the nuclear dream dissolved* (New York: Basic Books).

Collingridge, D. (1983), *Technology in the Policy Process: Controlling nuclear power* (London: Pinter).

Collins, H. (ed.) (1982), *Sociology of Scientific Knowledge: A source book* (Bath: Bath University Press).

Collins, H. (1985), *Changing Order: Replication and induction in scientific practise* (Beverly Hills, CA: Sage).

Collins, H. (1986), The core set and the public experiment. Unpublished manuscript.

Collins, H. M. (1988), Public experiments and displays of virtuosity: the core-set revisited; *Social Studies of Science*, 18, 725–48.

Conrad, J. (1982), Scientific expertise in technological controversies: the nuclear and recombinant DNA debates; *International Political Science Review*, 3, 315–1, 322.

Divine, R.A. (1978), *Blowing On the Wind: The Nuclear Test Ban debate, 1954–1960* (New York: Oxford University Press).

Fallows, S. (1979), The nuclear waste disposal controversy; in Nelkin, D. (ed.)
    Controversy: Politics of technical decisions (Beverly Hills, CA: Sage); 87–110,
    2nd rev. edn 1984.
Fischoff, B., Lichtenstein, S., Slovic, P., Derby, S. L. and Keeney, R. L. (1981),
    Acceptable Risk (Cambridge: Cambridge University Press).
Ford, D. (1984), *The Cult of the Atom: The secret papers of the Atomic Energy
    Commission* (New York: Simon & Schuster).
Gofman, J. and Tamplin, A. (1971), *Poisoned Power: The case against nuclear power
    plants* (Emmaus, PA: Rodale Press).
Guedeney, C. and Mendel, G. (1973), *L'angoisse atomique et les centrales nucléaires
    [Atomic Fear and Nuclear Power Stations]* (Paris: Payot).
Häfele, W. (1974), Hypotheticality and the new challenges: the pathfinder role of nuclear
    energy; *Minerva*, 12, 303–22.
Knorr-Cetina, K. and Mulkay, M. (eds) (1983), *Science Observed: Perspectives on the
    social study of science* (Beverly Hills, CA: Sage).
Kopp, C. (1979), The origins of the American scientific debate over fallout hazards;
    Social Studies of Science, 9, 403–22.
Kuhn, T.S. (1962), *The Structure of Scientific Revolutions* (Chicago, IL: Chicago
    University Press).
Latour, B. (1987), *Science in Action: How to follow scientists and engineers through
    society* (Milton Keynes: Open University Press).
Latour, B. and Woolgar, S. (1986), *Laboratory Life: The construction of scientific facts,*
    2nd edn (Princeton, NJ: Princeton University Press).
Lewis, R.S. (1973), *The Nuclear Power Rebellion: Citizens vs. the atomic industrial
    establishment* (New York: Viking Press).
Lowe, P. and Rüdig, W. (1986), Political ecology and the social sciences – the state of the
    art; *British Journal of Political Science*, 16, 513–50.
MacKenzie, D. and Wajcman, J. (eds) (1985), *The Social Shaping of Technology* (Milton
    Keynes: Open University Press).
MacKenzie, D., Rüdig, W. and Spinardi, G. (1988), Social research on technology and
    the policy agenda: an example from the strategic arms race; in Elliott, B. (ed.)
    Technology and Social Process (Edinburgh: Edinburgh University Press).
Mazur, A. (1981), *The Dynamics of Technical Controversy* (Washington, DC:
    Communications Press).
Nelkin, D. (1971), *Nuclear Power and its Critics: The Cayuga Lake controversy*
    (Ithaca, NY: Cornell University Press).
Nelkin, D. (1975), The political impact of technical expertise; *Social Studies of Science*,
    5, 35–54.
Nowotny, H. (1977), Scientific purity and nuclear danger: The case of risk-assessment; in
    Mendelsohn, E., Weingart, P. and Whitley, R. (eds) *The Social Production of Scientific
    Knowledge* (Sociology of the Sciences, Vol. 1) (Dordrecht: Reidel).
Nowotny, H. (1979), *Kernenergie: Gefahr oder Notwendigkeit [Nuclear Energy: Danger
    or necessity]* (Frankfurt: Suhrkamp).
Nowotny, H. and Hirsch, H. (1980), The consequences of dissent: sociological reflections
    on the controversy of the low dose effect; *Research Policy*, 9, 278–94.
Patterson, W. (1976), *Nuclear Power* (Harmondsworth: Penguin).
Perrow, C. (1984), *Normal Accidents: Living with high-risk technologies* (New York:
    Basic Books).
Perry *et al.* (1977), *Development and Commercialization of the Light Water Reactor,
    1946–1976* (Santa Monica, CA: RAND Corporation).
Primack, J. and Hippel, F. van (1974), *Advice and Dissent: Scientists in the political
    arena* (New York: Basic Books).

Rolph, E. S. (1979), *Nuclear Power and the Public Safety: A study in regulation* (Lexington, MA: Lexington Books).

Rüdig, W. (1988), Outcomes of nuclear technology policy: do varying political styles make a difference?; *Journal of Public Policy, 7*, 389–430.

Rüdig, W. (1989), *Towards a 'New' Political Science of Technology* (Strathclyde Papers in Government and Politics, No. 63) (Glasgow: Department of Government, University of Strathclyde).

Rüdig, W. (1990), *Anti-Nuclear Movements: A world survey of opposition to nuclear energy* (Harlow: Longman).

Rüdig, W. (1991), *The Green Wave: A comparative analysis of ecological parties* (Cambridge: Polity Press).

Sivadon, P. and Fernandez, A. (1968), *L'études des attitudes psychologiques des travailleurs nucléaire vis-à-vis des risques radioactifs [Study of the Psychological Attitudes of Nuclear Workers on Radioactive Risks]* (Brussels: EURATOM).

Sternglass, E. J. (1973), *Low Level Radiation* (London: Earth Island).

Ullrich, O. (1979), *Weltniveau. In der Sackgasse des Industriesystems [World Standard: In the cul-de-sac of the industrial system]* (Berlin: Rotbuch Verlag).

Weinberg, A. M. (1972a), Science and trans-science; *Minerva, 10*, 209–22.

Weinberg, A. M. (1972b), Social institutions and nuclear energy; *Science, 177*, 27–34.

Three

Chernobyl Comes to Italy
The Reciprocal Relationships of Radiation Experts, Government Policies and the Mass Media

ANGELA LIBERATORE

This chapter offers obvious empirical interest in its choice of study: the Italian Government's reaction to the effects of Chernobyl. The outline account separates Government, expert advisers and mass media activity in order to clarify these three elements. It goes on to offer and discuss a hypothesis that all three have a reciprocal relationship which has some very important consequences for making the political and governmental systems somewhat more open and accountable, even during a potentially catastrophic emergency, than they otherwise would be. By bringing in the mass media and their linkage with expert advisers, Angela Liberatore runs rather wider than the other authors and serves the valuable purpose of setting 'expert advice to governments' into a wider political background. The chapter begins with some academic context concerning decision-making and the concept of 'trans-science'.

Concerning the Italian case study, it is worth noting that many, or all, other countries affected by Chernobyl were claimed to have had the weaknesses of their protection systems shown up by these unprecedented events (Gould 1990; Park 1989). In Britain, certainly, the most bitter exchanges have continued, notably about the Ministry of Agriculture's alleged delays in acting and the existence of radioactive 'hot spots' in some rural areas from which farm animals have continued to be raised, slaughtered and eaten, to the possible public danger. Differences between official and unofficial (university) estimates of continuing radioactivity were as much as forty-fold in early 1989. Many readers of Angela Liberatore's chapter may well reflect on her point that Italian pluralism in ministries' emergency functions may have some advantage compared with a well-ordered official system in which the sole designated agency has the monopoly power possibly to be quite wrong in its conclusion.

INTRODUCTION

This chapter reviews what happened when an unexpected and unprecedented national threat suddenly faced a particular set of governmental arrangements (laws and technical capacities) which had been assembled over the years. These arrangements had been devised incrementally and without a coherent plan, mainly because of the rival political and economic interests lying behind them which the state promoted or represented to some extent. Some general theoretical considerations when considering expert technical advice in the setting of institutional power are first outlined. The Italian Government's provisions for monitoring and protecting against radiation poisoning are reviewed, with their various weaknesses. A brief account of the Chernobyl emergency in Italy follows. It distinguishes what Government bodies did and said from some of the mass media's and experts' comments and information. The chapter concludes with a discussion of the triangular relationship between expert advice, government decisions and the role of the mass media, following a particular hypothesis or theoretical pathway. This suggests that the relationships between the three sides of this triangle are reciprocally influenced. In particular, the importance of expert advice and the mass media for each other – and their joint effect on the government – deserves emphasis.

EXPERT ADVICE AND INSTITUTIONAL POWER

The need for both science and politics to live with uncertainty is well known since both uncontested scientific 'truths' and political decisions taken with perfect, 'rational' knowledge are both very rare. But some scientific uncertainties can precipitate political issues and give decision-makers a chance to choose between, or even to manipulate, scientific sources. In high-risk technology fields, honest expert disagreement can arise from the need to discuss unverifiable probabilities rather than traditional 'facts' (Otway 1987). Such discussions soon raise 'trans-scientific' questions (Weinberg 1972) which can be stated but cannot be solved by scientific terms and procedures: scientists are not, therefore, specially equipped on the ultimate questions involved. Perhaps the borderline into 'trans-science' is less precise than Weinberg may have suggested, but the question is who should decide where to draw it by deciding which issues are not only scientific but ultimately political – and how should this be done? Some expert controversies which spill over from what is (too loosely) known as 'the scientific community' do so because a political solution, as well as a technical one, is being sought. Here, institutional power as well as scientific explanations is involved (Jasanoff 1987).

Institutional power over expert information sources can be used to select information so that the political decision-maker may 'know' (and let be known to others) only enough to support, but not to challenge, existing institutional policies or goals. He does not desire – and certainly wants to keep from others – more knowledge than he thinks it is good to be known. This contrived 'half-knowledge' (Lazarsfeld 1967; Marin 1981) is less prey to uncertainties and disagreements among experts because it is deliberately stunted, but it is not immune to them. They may be experienced in the course of obtaining even 'half-knowledge'; some scientific issues are uncertain at any level. In any event, the decision-maker will have much information which is uncertain. Then it may be the decision-making procedures far more than the substance of the information itself which determine an outcome. If knowledge is scarce or uncertain, the outcome may well be that which best fits the procedures selected (Simon 1976). How is expert advice taken into such decision processes and by whom?

It would be too simple to say that experts are only ever used by political decision-makers for legitimating, but it is a commonplace occurrence. One explanation (Brickman *et al.* 1985) points to the vulnerability of some ministers and public officials whose goals may be quite readily destroyed by their political superiors, by legislators or the courts. In the US case, for example, concerning many controversial and often vulnerable decisions by regulatory commissions, the main defence is to have plenty of scientific evidence on display. This is more authoritative in a political culture which respects 'science' a lot more than it does civil servants. Even when decision-makers feel less vulnerable, having plenty of technical information on hand can encourage a technocratic approach which claims that only experts can consider such complexities. But experts may not be used only as legitimators. Experts may help to define problems, to choose the procedures for decision, evaluate the information and settle the range of possible outcomes. Even if they may, in some cases, then be formally excluded from the the the choice of outcome, their input would already have influenced that outcome. Their role would be stronger when this initial information is needed for an actual decision rather than sought to be a cosmetic or legitimating feature of the decision (or non-decision) already taken. And if the decision process in question is ill-defined the experts' contribution can be particularly important in shaping its definition and its possible solutions.

AN UNCERTAIN SYSTEM: LAW AND ADMINISTRATION FOR PUBLIC EMERGENCIES IN ITALY

The Chernobyl disaster found an Italian legal and governmental framework for radiation safety as such – and for public emergencies or disasters as such – which was incomplete, overlapping and unclear. In setting it out, one must begin with the law which, with its deficiencies, had to serve as the main legal reference point for the management of the Chernobyl emergency: the Presidential Decree 185 of 1964. It also dealt with the authorization of siting of nuclear plants, but only its radiation and monitoring aspects will arise here. It made four State organizations responsible, in different ways, for these tasks: the nuclear plant operator, the Ministry of Health, the Ministry of Industry and ENEA (National Committee for Nuclear and Alternative Energy), which is the nuclear industry's promoter body. The nuclear power plant operator (the State monopoly electricity producer, ENEL) is required to provide permanent monitoring of radioactive levels in water, soil, food and the air (art. 57). Naturally, ENEL owns this equipment and some dispute arose when it was building the nuclear plant at Caorso. It was decided that the local government health authorities would be allowed to study ENEL's measurements and to take their own (Schiavi 1987; Spaziante 1980).

The Ministry of Health (through its technical agents) must control, including by inspection, radioactive sources to protect the health of both workers affected by the radiation and the public (arts. 88 and 109). It has a standing advisory body in this field: the National Institute of Health (ISS). The ISS is charged (under Law 519 of 1973) with research into all aspects of public health protection and may investigate health standards at work and at large. ISS representatives have often openly criticized Italian procedures for authorizing and siting nuclear plants and the emergency plans which are produced. For example, they did so in 1975 at a conference on energy development organized by the Umbria regional government. The accident at Three Mile Island strengthened ISS's case but did not prevent an assault on its powers by the Ministry of Industry, acting as the promoter of the State electricity (including nuclear) producer, ENEL. Under Law 833 of 1978, ISS was prevented from giving advice on health standards for the production of nuclear power or radioactive substances (art. 9). The Minister of Industry told the *Corriere della Sera* (6 January 1979) that ISS should withdraw in order to end an overlap of functions with ENEA as a monitoring agency. One interpretation (Spaziante 1980) was that ISS was punished for its critical views on the nuclear power industry. ISS's functions were later given to ISPESL (the National Institute of Work Prevention and Safety) but this body lacked the equipment and staff to perform them. As a result, ISS was continuing this work, despite the disabling law of 1978, but only on an *ad hoc* and terminal basis. When Chernobyl exploded, ISS was still in place in this field but on this odd and legally uncertain basis.

The Ministry of Industry commands important resources on nuclear safety because of its legal supervision of ENEA, the National Committee for Nuclear and Alternative Energy. ENEA must follow the Ministry of Industry's directions in co-ordinating and promoting all radioactivity monitoring towards the goal of a single national network (art. 109); it must also convey Italian data to the ECC Commission in Brussels. ENEA is a notable example of institutional ambiguity, thanks to its historical background.

Previously called CNEN (National Council for Nuclear Energy) under Law 933 of 1960, ENEA had a stormy career which reflected the fluctuations of Italian nuclear power policy. After serious problems in the 1960s (due in part to the opposition of the powerful oil lobby to CNEN's attempts to promote a national nuclear power industry) the agency underwent a first restructuring in 1974. In that year a partial attempt was made to separate the nuclear power promotion and regulation functions attributed to CNEN by establishing a Safety and Protection Division (DISP) within the agency. But this division did not receive a legal identity and autonomy either at once in 1974, or even eight years later when Law 84 of 1982 was passed, turning CNEN into its modern form of ENEA. An associated Law (85, 1982) still provided for the Director of ENEA-DISP to be appointed by the Ministry of Industry which also controls the budget of the Division. In this way the ministerial sponsor of the nuclear industry (nationalized in 1962) also directly controls the regulatory body.

After the anti-nuclear referendum held in November 1987, ENEA and ENEA-DISP are undergoing a further – and quite confusing – restructuring.

Four legally responsible, executive bodies on radiation protection and monitoring – the plant operator (ENEL); the Ministry of Health with its ISS agency; the nuclear industry's promoter body (ENEA) in association with DISP, and the local health units (USLs) – were the country's official guardians against radiation poisoning when Chernobyl came to Italy. In addition, some academic or other laboratories had some equipment and expertise and some local governments had also begun local testing. A leading academic laboratory was the IFA (the Atmospheric Physics Institute) of the CNR (Council for National Research); the Council's president testified later at the Chamber of Deputies' inquiry into the Chernobyl episode. The Minister of Health also enjoys legal powers (under art. 88 of the same presidential decree, DPR 185 / 1964) over the operations of the Ministry of Home Affairs and the provincial prefect when a nuclear power accident may affect more than one Province. The prefect is required to establish a committee within the Province and to co-ordinate the provincial emergency plan (art. 18). He is to promote public safety in this event (art. 122). He must report to the Ministry of Home Affairs any radioactive emission which threatens the public and that Ministry must then follow the Ministry of Health's requirements on the protection of either the public or nuclear workers from radiation danger. Although the technical standards, and perhaps also the actual measures, to be taken by the Ministry of Home Affairs and the prefectures are specified by the Ministry of Health, it would seem that the law grants the central executive role to the Ministry of Home Affairs. But, as we shall see, the Ministry of Health took direct legal measures during the Chernobyl period.

This is the Italian legal and governmental framework for dealing with the risks of radioactivity poisoning, and there are already two departments – Health and Home Affairs – which may claim the leading role. If we transfer our attention to the national framework for dealing with emergencies and catastrophes – of whatever type – a different picture is to be seen. Another Department (not yet even mentioned), the Ministry of Civil Protection, now appears centre stage because of Law 938 of 1982. It is responsible for mounting 'urgent interventions on behalf of populations hit by natural calamities and exceptional events'. It establishes that the Ministry of Civil Protection may take steps to intervene, having consulted those Regional governments – covering a number of Provinces – which are involved. (As will also be seen, this Ministry took responsibility for certain key initial executive actions at the outset of the Chernobyl disaster period.) This Ministry also contains two standing bodies whose members include other Departments' and agencies' representatives who jointly convey to it their own departmental colleagues' views and actions about the threat in question. These two bodies are the CGR (High Risks Commission) and EMERCOM (Operative Committee for Emergencies). The CGR advises the Ministry of Civil Protection on six types of public risk, including nuclear radiation. Under a decree of 1986 its nuclear group comprises the directors of the monitoring bodies we have noted: ENEA-DISP, the ISS and ISPESL (Work Prevention and Security) plus two university professors. EMER-

COM has representatives of the Ministries of Agriculture, Defence, Health, Home Affairs, Navy, Public Works, Telecommunications and Transport. It was set up in 1984 to assist the Ministry of Civil Protection to deal with public calamities.

Three potentially 'leading' Ministries, supported by their respective agencies and advisory bodies, were to be confronted by the unprecedented Chernobyl threat. From this simple layout of these bodies' names and relevant functions, it is clear that weaknesses of response would be expected. In particular, Italian law and public administration had not provided for a radiation emergency which was either of external origin or of simultaneous national effect – and Chernobyl was, of course, both. Italy, like many other countries with nuclear stations on its own territory, had legislated for only the risk of an Italian station producing a serious or catastrophic emission. So both the scale and the basis of the actual Chernobyl experience was different from the ones for which the law and administrative structure might otherwise have claimed to be prepared.

THE UNEXPECTED EMERGENCY: CHERNOBYL IN ITALY AND ITS AFTERMATH

In the late afternoon of 28 April 1986, the first news reached Italy indirectly that the Swedes were reporting more than a doubling of their normal background radioactivity. That evening the USSR reported an incident at Chernobyl to the International Atomic Energy Authority. Figure 3.1 gives an account set out in the form of two simultaneous sequences, of what was done or said by the Italian Government bodies, the mass media and certain experts.

It has been argued that Italy had no formal and legally-based emergency because the atmospheric radiation reached only the 'attention threshold', not the 'danger threshold' level (ENEA-DISP 1986). But vegetables in the North did contain enough Iodine 131 (and those in the Centre nearly enough) to reach the formal emergency level (ISS 1987). This question of the legality of official action was entwined around much other argument on the recent events. The Ministry of Health and its ISS (working on monitoring with ENEA-DISP) had fallen out with Agriculture and Industry (whose Minister appoints the director of ENEA) because of their different national responsibilities: public health and economic promotion. Each Department and agency had cause to worry if events proved that its public position had been wrong. If its countermeasures proved completely pointless, the Health Ministry could lose public legitimacy and influence within the Cabinet; and its ISS could lose both public and scientific credibility. But if the anti-emergency views of other Ministries such as Industry and Agriculture had prevailed and many people had died or become ill as a consequence, then they, together with ENEA, ENEA-DISP and the already controversial nuclear industry, would run into serious difficulties. All those favouring nuclear power development perceived the risk of losing legitimacy and public funding if mass opposition to nuclear power spread as a consequence of the Chernobyl accident (whether countermeasures were taken or not) and caused further damage to the already unstable Italian nuclear power industry.

Figure 3.1 Government and mass media public expert responses to Chernobyl

	Government	Mass Media	Public expert advice
28 April	The Ministry of Civil Protection consulted the official executive agencies for radioactive monitoring: the ISS and ENEA-DISP. It also, as a precaution, called a meeting of both CGR (High Risks Commission) and EMERCOM (representing eight other Ministries) for the next day. The Minister of Civil Protection (G. Zamberletti) and the Director of ENEA-DISP (G. Naschi) told the press that Italian levels were normal and that the higher levels were expected to affect only Northern Europe. Some Northern Italian monitor points already showed higher atmospheric levels of radiation (Naschi 1987).		
29 April	The CGR and EMERCOM decided to check all Italian monitoring equipment readings, ENEA, ENEL (the State electricity board) CNR (National Research Council) the Air Force, etc. (Some days later, eleven universities and several other bodies and companies were also required to intensify and report their readings). An *ad hoc* technical commission was established to evaluate the readings: members from ENEA-DISP, ISS, Home Affairs,Civil Protection and Defence comprised this body.	The morning papers reported a serious accident at Chernobyl and reported the Zamberletti and Naschi statements.	On TV, the Italian Nobel laureate physicist, C. Rubbia, warned that Chernobyl could be a meltdown with serious and wide-scale consequences.
30 April	Laboratories at Piacenza and Bologna reported appreciable increases in radioactivity. G. Zamberletti repeated his optimistic view in the Senate: the Italian situation was 'under control'. The radioactive cloud would affect only Northern Italy, perhaps during 1–3 May, and be no risk to the population. The Minister for Industry, R. Altissimo, was even more optimistic in the Chamber of Deputies. Both Ministers stressed the lack of Soviet information but did not allow this ignorance of the nature of the threat to dent their positive views.	The chance of a meltdown was a major story although no precise information was yet available from USSR. Some newspapers reported up to 2000 deaths.	
1 May	All stations reported further increases of radioactivity in the air, rain water and soil, particularly in the North. The Chernobyl cloud was officially said to be over North Italy.	The increasing Italian radioactivity and Zamberletti's reassuring statements were both reported.	

2 May	Government special measures began with the Ministry of Public Protection requiring the confidential, centralized collection of all monitoring results, for its exclusive publication. This was in the form of 'daily average estimates' for each of three large aggregated areas: North, Central and South Italy. The motives were practical (daily collection and dissemination from many monitor stations) and political (avoiding panic near the highest reading places; discounting public concern about nuclear power and existing Italian stations). The Ministry of Health (on advice from its technical agency, ISS) decreed a ban on selling fresh broad-leaved vegetables and giving fresh milk to under-tens and to pregnant women.	Agitated reporting of arguments on these bans; the dangers they indicated; whom should be believed or trusted in the Government. Mass media comment by those who thoughtGovernment actions excessive or, alternatively, wholly inadequate.	Some scientists (and the Greens) said the broad-based average radiation readings concealed very high readings ('hot spots') and covered only Iodine 131 and Cesium 137, ignoring other toxic elements (De Sanctis 1986). The mass media and experts were both confused by the use in the collection and publication of readings of both the Curie (Ci) and Becquerel (Bq) measurement systems.
3 May	Some local governments tried to add extra advice and bans, such as against children playing on grass. The Ministries of Agriculture and Industry accused Health of exaggerating the danger and so damaging farmers, traders and economic life.		
5 May	The secretary of the Cabinet met with the Ministers of Agriculture, Civil Protection, Health and Industry: the Ministry of Health decree was not revoked. The Minister of Industry (the promoter of the nuclear power industry) tells the Chamber of Deputies that Italian plants are quite different from Chernobyl's design and implies that they are wholly safe.		

6 May		A long, careful TV documentary concludes with the Ministers of Health and Civil Protection; the director of ENEA-DISP (the co-ordinating agency for radiation monitoring); the Greens' leader, G. Mattioli (a physicist); and several other scientists. A veteran physicist and nuclear power adherent attacked Mattioli fiercely.
7 May	The Ministry of Health refined the terms of its measures in two further ordinances. The Ministry of Industry discussed ECC trade problems arising from the disaster with relevant firms. In the Chamber of Deputies the Communist Party demanded a review of Italian nuclear power policy.	Reports of a news conference (where the Radicals, Democratic Proletarian and Green parties proposed a national referendum on nuclear power) and of left-wing parliamentary motions to close at once the Latina nuclear plant; control more closely the others; improve emergency plans; establish a national agency on high risks; and call a national energy conference.
10 May	The President of the Republic seeks clarification on radioactivity contamination from Ministers and experts.	The press reported polemics about data concerning radioactivity levels.
11 May		Reports of 150–200,000 demonstrators in Rome 'yesterday' opposing nuclear power, showing that this view was not that of only small Left or Green groups.
17 May	The fifteen-day period of the vegetable and milk bans expired and was not extended.	
20 May	The Emergency was ended with satisfied comments by the Ministers of Civil Protection and Health about the efficiency and prudence displayed during the previous 27 days.	

Arising from much argument after 'Chernobyl', notably, of course, on long-term health consequences, four main outcomes should be mentioned. They are the controversial National Conference on Energy, held in Rome in February 1987; the national referendum on nuclear power, held in November 1987, which produced an adverse result; and the continuing debates about setting up a national agency on high risks and about splitting ENEA-DISP from ENEA to give it a quite distinct and legally autonomous role as a specialist safety body.

SCIENTISTS, GOVERNMENT AND MASS MEDIA
A THEORETICAL PATHWAY

This analysis of the Chernobyl radiation emergency in Italy focuses on three key elements of the theme of 'expert advice to governments'. They are: the questions of what the scientific experts select as relevant knowledge and information – this requires a review of the sources of policy advice on radiation safety; what politicians wished to learn of this material and wished to let the public know – this entails asking how information from experts was used by the public authorities to help manage the Chernobyl emergency in an unclear and fragmented structure whose definition and co-ordination of political responsibilities were both poor; and what the mass media learn of it and decide to stress or minimize in their reporting – this question raises the issue of news marketing but is also linked back to the scientific experts because they inform the media as well as the Government with their expert analyses and judgments. These three elements obviously stand closely together but the hypothesis proposed here is that they also reciprocally influence each other; they must therefore be viewed together as well as described separately.

A simple theoretical pathway which attempts to do this might be along these lines. Experts' advice is usually required by governments in order to help make a pending decision or merely to legitimate one already made. This advice may be either generally agreed or controversial among other relevant experts. It may also include substantive or conceptual uncertainties (because the 'state of the art' is imperfect) which may be made explicit or kept hidden from the adviser's client. If kept hidden, this may be done deliberately by an adviser who realizes the inherent limitations of the material, concepts or techniques which the 'state of the art' currently offers, or it may be done unconsciously by an adviser who does not realize these things. Turning to the official government clients for this expert advice, their own technical and political authority may be well- or ill-defined. Different Departments and agencies within the government can have overlapping or conflicting competences in a field such as energy policy depending on their different tasks (for example, industry promotion *versus* environmental health protection). Therefore it can be difficult to find out which Department is principally responsible for decisions. In order to overcome this institutional uncertainty, especially on complex technical issues, expert committees are often appointed. But these committees may disagree with the Department and so produce new uncertainties. A vicious circle could result: because of institutional uncertainty on complex issues, expert advice is requested but expert disagreements and cognitive uncertainty may emerge and increase the institutional uncertainty and the need for supplementary advice. The circle can be broken by the emergence of actors able to affirm their authority thanks to economic, technical or legal resources or to their better performance in coalition and bargaining processes.

Let us now try to link this theoretical pathway with the chronicle of the Chernobyl emergency sketched above. The Chernobyl catastrophe showed that even very unlikely events can occur, even possibly 'tomorrow'. But such events enjoy only low legislative and administrative priority so an inadequate public emergency plan would be no surprise. One official reaction might, hypothetically, be to try to hide or ignore the unwelcome event or, at least, to discount its importance. A government might hope the problem will be only brief or less serious than it may have feared. The USSR and French Governments tried this initial reaction to Chernobyl because nuclear power promotion is very important *à propos* both of them and because of their highly centralized bureaucratic structure. But international communications (particularly, on this matter, satellite surveys and exchanges of data between radiation monitors and interested scientists in many countries) made this suppression of the event impossible. The approaching cloud revived at once the familiar international controversy of whether there is a threshold dose for radiation (below which no effects occur) and whether long-term, low-dose exposure is harmful. Each affected country took particular measures according to its location in Europe, its governmental and political system and its relevant scientific resources. It has been hypothesized above that there are reciprocal influences at work between scientists, politicians and the mass media within each country's particular institutional setting. In considering this hypothesis, three aspects of the Italian Chernobyl experience deserve attention:

1. The collection, selection and use of technical information by the policy advisers.
2. The policy-makers' use of it for managing the emergency.
3. The mass media's role in communication problems between these two élite groups and the citizens.

(1) The policy advisers

As we have seen, the technical agencies were brought together by the Ministry of Civil Protection into an *ad hoc* commission to report and advise daily on radiation data. But they had their differences and also operated separately. Their common problem was inadequate information, initially from the USSR about the explosion itself and then from different types and qualities of Italian monitor instruments which offered a seriously incomplete picture. There were fewer instruments in the South and on the Adriatic and Islands and some radioactive elements could not be widely monitored at all. Then there were the problems of measurement methods and scales which we have already noted. This bad practical position may have encouraged some of the technical commission to argue that something serious had happened at Chernobyl but to claim or hope that little would happen in Italy as a result. This attitude may have been the specific basis for the optimistic immediate public statements of the Ministers of Industry and Civil Protection. Other experts took the bad practical provision for monitoring as an added reason for a vigorous precautionary policy to protect public health: it would be prudent to assume the worst. The vegetable and milk bans, referring to Iodine 131 and Cesium 137, were decided upon this basis. Familiar scientific arguments on safe thresholds and low-dosage effects were dramatically revived and different positions asserted (ENEA-DISP 1986; ISS 1987). The Ministries of Industry and Agriculture adopted the more optimistic of these two schools of thought to attack the Government's destruction of stocks of vegetables, milk and other foods as unnecessarily wasteful. How could it be justified if the experts were so divided on the scientific issue? In contrast, the Ministry of Health and its ISS agency believe that the more doubt as to the facts, the more prudence should be applied to policy. They could claim to be following the International Commission on Radiological Pollution's standards.

(2) The policy-makers

Clearly, political management questions overlaid scientific ones from the outset, as international comparisons reveal. With similar radiation levels, Italy, Austria, The Netherlands and Federal Germany did ban the sale of broad-leaved vegetables while the other countries did not. Yet almost all banned the import of vegetables and some other foods. The differences were political, not scientific. Italy's Ministry of Health had a fairly clear legal power to act on public health issues, whereas Government powers and allocations of responsibility to react to a public emergency in general (of whatever type) are seriously deficient. The Ministry of Civil Protection, with its broader role on emergencies and catastrophes, took this clear public health jurisdiction into account. The Ministry of Health was also fortunate to have as its exclusive agency the recognized and internationally connected Italian scientific authority on radiation, the ISS. Its position on prudential actions was almost certainly vital in the Ministry of Health holding the line against its critics in the Cabinet.

(3) The mass media

The mass media crucially shaped the Chernobyl emergency in Italy. In their nature, mass media will disseminate and even magnify existing differences of analysis or opinion among both the experts and the political policy-makers. They should not be blamed for simply reporting the divisions of others (although they often are – and were so criticized in Italy). Members of élites who think they understand problems and 'facts' often claim that the mass media feeds the public's 'irrational' fears: but during 'Chernobyl' no person could honestly claim to know where 'irrational' fears began. Because the danger from radiation is invisible, the mass media had a main role in making it visible by using words such as radioactivity, iodine 131, meltdown and cancer and by showing photographs and documentaries about nuclear plants and the fire at Chernobyl. Moreover, the emergency had been publicly defined by the mass media's reporting of confusing data on the concentration of radioactive elements in food and by governmental prohibitions and recommendations on certain foodstuffs. In many cases the quality of mass media information was quite bad due to the complexity of the issues but also due to the attempt to produce 'marketable' news.

But these elements are not sufficient to conclude that the reporting of the Chernobyl fall-out had a merely informative nature because it was perceived by the public only by means of newspapers, radio and television (Pierantoni 1987). Nor can Chernobyl be seen as merely a matter of opinion because lay people had no knowledge of 'objective facts' (Minerva 1986). It was clear to lay people that something serious had happened that endangered the life of many people in the Ukraine; that an invisible cloud full of a dangerous 'substance' was moving about in Europe; that some quantities of that 'substance' were in the air, soil and water of Italy; that scientists disagreed about the possible danger of breathing and ingesting even small quantities of that 'substance'; and that the authorities had ordered them not to sell and eat some foods.

This was the evidence – not invented by the journalists – available to lay people and it was not irrational but very reasonable to have some fears on the basis of such evidence. These fears had to be taken into account by experts and politicians in the management of the emergency. Here the communication role of the mass media becomes evident: scientists and politicians were not allowed to discuss and decide in isolation and secrecy. Even if the gate-keepers of information tried to select what to let out, they could not really control all the official and unofficial sources of information in Italy and abroad. In particular they could not control the quality of the news and its impact on the public. This partially public dimension of both the scientific debate and the political decision-making process influenced their shape and output.

The extensive media coverage of the Chernobyl event and the connected issues certainly influenced the debate between scientific experts by providing public room for critical views. This exposure in turn influenced Government policy-makers who realized that their actions and words would be fully examined in a forum beyond their control. Not only Italian data, events and opinions would be on display to a worried public but also equivalent information from other affected countries. This exposure and consequent accountability influenced the political management of the Chernobyl emergency so that a fairly prudent approach to public health precautions prevailed over immediate economic calculations.

CONCLUSION

In concluding this review, it must first be noted that the cognitive and institutional uncertainty experienced during the Chernobyl emergency would have been very similar in type, if not in scale, if an Italian (or Italian border) nuclear power station had offered a similar disastrous threat. This would apply particularly to the inadequate monitoring and reporting system and the ambiguous emergency powers. Since 'Chernobyl' the monitoring points have been extended but the emergency plan is still deficient. Research and regulation in low level radiation doses, radioactive waste transport or storage and nuclear plant decommissioning is also still neglected. These continuing weaknesses reveal that very unlikely accidents receive low political priority, despite their possibly huge potential risk, probably because it is unthinkingly assumed that unlikely accidents will always happen well into the future, if at all, and never 'tomorrow' (Perrow 1984). As to the ambiguous Government powers and roles, they could have paralysed ministers afraid to act *ultra vires* perhaps on another ministry's 'patch'. Instead, this seems to have encouraged them to assert and confirm their poorly defined 'patches' by acting quite boldly. Such a pluralism of ministers' possible powers, while creating costs in co-ordination and implementation, may be preferable to a tightly defined system which puts the powers in the wrong place – for example, monitoring and safety standards powers in a ministry whose political priority is to promote the polluting industry in question, particularly the nuclear power industry.

In a disaster of this novel type expert information is of essential importance. As the political success of the Ministry of Health in getting and keeping its bans against governmental critics showed, the possession and analysis of legitimate technical information is of the essence. The extensive mass media coverage of the Chernobyl experience prevented any official attempts to hide uncertainty or expert disagreements while claiming to the public that 'everything is under control'. Independent mass media provide the means to a more open system of government decision-making because their demands for information and their public reports help break down the popular view of 'science' as either objective or omnicompetent. The greater danger arises when expert technical advice which is thought to be sound goes into a government decision system without a public challenge and proves in fact to have been wrong or seriously inadequate.

It seems clear from a consideration of 'Chernobyl' in Italy that relationships between expert information, government decisions and mass media exposure are, indeed, reciprocal. The existence of the others affects the operation of each. The point which deserves particular emphasis is that the expert – mass media relationship is as important as the other two sides of the triangle because it will help to make the public authorities more open and accountable than they would otherwise be seriously tempted to be. This is perhaps particularly so in the uniquely difficult and controversial fields of nuclear power and radiation-based technology with their continuous threat of causing extremely long-term poisoning of the population.

Brickman, R., Jasanoff, S. and Ilgen, T. (1985), *Controlling Chemicals: The politics of regulation in Europe and the United States* (Ithaca, NY: Cornell University Press).
De Sanctis, V. (1986), Dossier Chernobyl; *Essere Terrestre,* 11–12
ENEA-DISP (1986), *The Chernobyl Incident: Radiological consequences in Italy – Report of 27 May 1986* (Rome: ENEA-DISP).
Gould, P. (1990), *Fire in the Rain: The democratic consequences of Chernobyl* (Cambridge: Polity Press).
ISS (1987), Annali dell'Instituto Superiore di Sanità, 23 February. Il rischio ambientale nella produzione di energia: risultati sperimentali, calcoli e riflessioni dopo Chernobyl [Annals of the ISS. Environmental risk in energy production: experimental results, calculations and reflections following Chernobyl]. Rome.

Jasanoff, S. (1987), Contested boundaries in policy-relevant science; *Social Studies of Science,* 17.
Lazarsfeld, P. (1967), Introduction; in Lazarsfeld, P.F., Sewell W.H. and Wilensky H.L. (eds), *The Uses of Sociology* (New York: Basic Books).
Marin, B. (1981), What is 'half-knowledge' sufficient for and when?; in *Knowledge: Creation, diffusion, utilization,* 3.1.
Minerva, D. (1986), Chernobyl è un' opinione?; *Sapere.*
Naschi, G. (1987), *Report of the Director of ENEA-DISP to the Minister of Industry for 1986* (Rome, ENEA-DISP).
Otway, H. (1987), Experts, risk communication and democracy; in *Risk Analysis,* 7.2.
Park, C. (1989), *Chernobyl: The long shadow* (London: Routledge).
Perrow, C. (1984), *Normal Accidents: Living with high risk technologies* (New York: Basic Books).
Pierantoni, F. (1987), Chernobyl: la sindrome televisiva [Chernobyl: the television syndrome]; *Il Mulino,* 1.
Schiavi, G.G. (1987), *Nucleare all'italiana [Nuclear Power in Italy]* (Milan: F. Angeli).
Simon, H. (1976), From substantive to procedural rationality; in Latsis, S.J. (ed.), *Methods and Appraisal in Economics* (Cambridge, MA: Cambridge University Press).
Spaziante, V. (1980), *Questione nucleare e politica legislativa [The Nuclear Question and Legislative Politics]* (Rome: Officina Edizioni).
Weinberg, A.M. (1972), Science and trans-science; *Minerva,* 10, 209–22.

Four

'Expert' and 'Political' Elements in Official Scientific Advice on Swiss Nuclear Power

CHRISTINE MIRONESCO

This comparison between two Swiss official committees of inquiry, both concerned with nuclear power, offers some neatly contrasting examples of the different forms, styles and types of authority which flow from the different kind of jobs to be done by each committee. Both were 'expert' but one also contrived to be politically representative, in the broad – not merely partisan – sense. The chapter shows well how wider social and cultural developments can overlay well-ordered constitutional and even governmental processes in a small, stable system such as Switzerland's. This system could not contain either the energy use – conservation or the economic growth – ecology issues: an 'alternative' and more radical-Left 'Global Energy Conception' report was published as a challenge to the official one, leaving the Swiss legislators and voters with the basic ideological choices. Apart from the other committee's mainly technical work on revising nuclear energy law, this chapter shows that some expert advice processes in scientific policy fields can do little more than clarify and arrange a series of issues which only voters and their political representatives can resolve. While familiar and even obvious in some political systems, this reality may cause dismay and strain in a system which has made maximum use of supposedly impartial technicians, not only to propose policy solutions but also to dispose of conflicts thereby.

INTRODUCTION

The importance of professionally trained people in modern political processes is widely recognized. However, many doubts remain concerning the exact part professionalism will play when it is necessary to take decisions. Ever since Weber, political theory has maintained that most developed countries were gradually moving from traditional to more rational types of political procedures. One misunderstanding born out of this intellectual tradition has been the 'end of ideology' school of thought. The idea was that the more decisions would be based on rationality, the less opportunities for conflict would occur in society, as if rational solutions could resolve all problems. Yet, at the end of the 1960s and the beginning of the 1970s, conflicts did appear in many industrialized countries and, curiously enough, they arose on issues which seemed to be highly technical and complex, such as energy. Today, public opinion seems somewhat more critical with regard to rationality in politics. But the role of professionals and experts is not very well known, although some research has been done (Nelkin 1977–1979, Nelkin & Pollack 1981; Germann 1981; Germann *et al.* 1986; Germann and Frutiger 1978). It is important to try to reach a better understanding of the question through case studies, not only in order to satisfy some theoretical curiosity but also on practical grounds: in order to improve the transparency of actual so-called technocratic decisions and to help to encourage a better-informed public.

THE SWISS CONTEXT

This outline of the Swiss political system focuses on some aspects which are relevant to our two expert committees. Switzerland's federal structure is reflected in the two-chamber Federal Assembly. It is composed of the National Council (200 members) representing the population directly and the Council of States (46 members) representing the canton administrations. The Federal Assembly is a non-professional, part-time parliament. Therefore, the average deputy is supposed sometimes to lack information and expertise on specific issues. This makes the parliament relatively weak in the decision-making process. On the other hand, the coexistence of the two legislative Councils clearly shows that both national and cantonal interests will be taken into account. Actually, on many traditional matters, there has been a clear division of powers between the federal government (the Federal Council) and the cantons. But, more recently and especially on energy issues, some ambiguities did appear. A case was recently submitted to the Federal Court; the controversy was about the siting of a nuclear plant in Verbois near Geneva. The Court ruled that the federal government was wrong to impose a nuclear plant on to a region against its will.

Swiss politics are well known as being shaped by interest groups (Kriesi 1980; Aubert 1978; Tschaeni 1983) and it is certainly true that bargaining procedures are extremely important. This does not mean, however, that the Federal Council and its administration is absent from the decision-making process. Its function in the consensus formation is important; it has a steering role in terms of preparing bills and mediating between divergent interests. Interest groups' powers and opportunities are also related to the even better-known Swiss emphasis on direct popular rights, notably the referendum and the popular initiative. All amendments of the federal constitution have to be submitted to a compulsory referendum. To pass, they must be approved by a majority of voters in the country as a whole in a majority of cantons. A popular initiative requires 100,000 valid signatures to induce a popular vote on an amendment of the constitution which was proposed by the initiative committee. It is sometimes a way of putting on the electoral agenda problems which had been neglected, such as energy and environmental issues. As a result of those popular rights, the pre-parliamentary process of decision is very important. In order to secure bills which have a chance of being accepted by the most important groups (those with so-called 'referendum capacities') the federal government organizes consultations among these groups and nominates expert committees to propose solutions. These expert committees have been labelled the 'militia administration' (Germann 1981). Although the expression seems to refer to non-professionals, it means that the experts are not professional administrators (like civil servants). But they do have professional skills which make them suitable for the task to which they have been assigned.

ENERGY POLICY AND THE STATE

The rise of the ecologist movements in most industrialized countries was associated with new values. A criticism of statism was one of them. However, this should not be understood, in the traditional way, as a defence of the free market mechanisms. It was rather a general distrust in regard to any excessive centralization related, for instance, to the implementation of large technologies (Inglehart 1977; Gorz 1978). On this particular point of view, Swiss ecologists seemed at first to go in the opposite direction: they demanded that the State should take a more active part in energy policy. There were reasons for such an attitude. Energy production belonged to the private sector. Environmental groups claimed that it was necessary to give power to the public authorities in order to control this private industry and – more generally – to control economic growth, to diversify resources, to encourage renewable energies and to make these decisions more transparent and politically accountable. The basic idea was to transform a technical issue into a political one. Leftist parties and political authorities soon supported this request (Schroeren 1977) and State intervention for the sake of greater national control became the central issue of the debates. Various and sometimes contradictory motivations appeared. The energy industry was originally against any such change but claimed after a while that it was in fact necessary to give more power to the central State as against the cantons, precisely because energy production was of technical and national concern and should not therefore be endangered by regional considerations. State intervention, as a counterweight to both the private sector and to cantonal power, was then discussed. Expert committees had to evaluate the degree and the type of State intervention needed and the benefits which might be expected from such an innovation.

CONFLICT RESOLUTION BY MEANS OF EXPERT COMMITTEES: A COMPARISON

Among the several expert committees which dealt with Swiss energy issues during those years, two are especially relevant for this analysis. Both were indeed responsible for the task of redefining the political rules of the game concerning State intervention. Although one of them had to do with global issues of Swiss energy policy while the other was limited to the nuclear power problem, it may prove fruitful to compare these committees for a better understanding of their relative characters.

It is difficult to assess the influence of these experts without any reference to the social and political setting in the country at the beginning of the 1970s. Expertise has various aspects, sources and expressions and there are clearly different ways of bringing it into play. In order to make the comparison more meaningful, we shall try to relate the work accomplished by those professionals to the conflict which provided the starting-point for current Swiss energy policy. To begin by considering this conflict is important here for two reasons. Firstly, conflict resolution is precisely the formal function of extra-parliamentary expert committees: they are significant in the decision-making process because of their role in consensus formation (Linder 1979). This function is sometimes criticized as being un-democratic, since the expert groups work in secret, behind the political scenes. Secondly, the nature of the conflict over energy policy shows what was at stake in the debates held by the committees. As in other industrialized western societies, the energy crisis seemed to have brought environmental problems into focus. The rapid and politically undisciplined economic growth had already been questioned, but the energy crisis enlarged the gap between the traditional representatives of the industrial sector and the ecologists. With the rather broad support of public opinion, ecological groups became organized and put some pressure on the government to bring about changes in energy policy, especially its production and distribution. This demand for better political control must be considered as really innovative: hitherto energy had generally been viewed as neither political (but purely technical) nor public (but belonging to the private sector).

Given this popular demand for policy innovation how do we evaluate the work accomplished by these experts? Which of the committees was more responsive or innovative? They were different in both their scope and their composition. They were similar, however, in being *ad hoc* committees and active during approximately the same period (c 1975–80) so it is rather easy to identify and compare their outputs. The comparison will offer no definite answer as to which committee proved more influential, but it does give clearer ideas about the part played by expert professionals, and about their relationship to politics and to civil society.

THE COMMITTEE FOR THE GLOBAL ENERGY CONCEPTION

The international oil price crisis of 1973 gave extra weight to the criticism of uncontrolled economic growth. In addition, Switzerland experienced events which were serious enough to compel the federal government to try to find national solutions for the energy problem. Opposition to nuclear power had grown, as in other countries. Besides an increasing general dissatisfaction with growth ideology and large technologies, there was also less confidence in the safety of nuclear plants and more concern for environmental problems resulting from industrialization. The opposition focused on the small community of Kaiseraugst, near Basle, where a nuclear plant had been granted a location licence by the Department of Traffic and

Energy. After a phase of legal protest – including petitions, information campaigns, publication of critical reports and lawsuits submitted to the federal Supreme Court – the opposition culminated in demonstrations and a sit-in of the construction site in Kaiseraugst. The planned nuclear plant was no longer a local issue. It became a question of national concern. It also cast a shadow on the legendary image of Swiss social peace.

When criticized for lacking a clear, general policy in energy matters, the federal government regularly answered that it had no legal basis for developing such a policy. But public pressure was high enough to promote the debate on only nuclear power issues to the broader level of a technocratic discussion on a global framework for Swiss energy policy. In 1974 the federal government (Federal Council) nominated an expert committee which was assigned to the task of drafting a 'global energy conception' (GEC). It was accepted from the very beginning, at least in principle, that this 'conception' should take into account the protection of the environment and the fact that resources were limited. The committee's report of 1978 recorded its terms of reference as: to define the country's objectives on energy policy; to evaluate the possible implementing of non-polluting technologies which allow the saving of resources; and to establish the measures necessary to attain these objectives.

The committee chose to present a number of options or scenarios. The idea was not to forecast the future, but to establish probable relationships expressed in the form of 'if ... then' propositions. These would show the likely connections between certain conditions and the results which might be expected for society if these conditions were in force over certain periods of time. State intervention was precisely at stake here. The conditions discussed by the experts and presented at length in the final report can be summarized as four scenarios for the government, politicians and citizens to consider. They were set out according to the degree of political intervention needed in order to diversify the sources of energy and to implement new policies. The four scenarios were as follows:

1. *Laissez-faire.*
2. *Some intervention* , in the sense of using all the existing legal bases including the cantons, which had rather more legal authority in this field than the federal government.
3. *More intervention* , involving a new constitutional article giving more power to the Confederation, including powers for legislation, possible taxes on energy use and so on. (This scenario was in fact composed of ten elements offering different levels of possible taxes and types of energy diversification which they might produce).
4. *Even more intervention* : this option was actually also named the 'stabilization' scenario because it was designed to halt the increase in energy consumption and production. The proposal had been studied and promoted by representatives of national ecological associations.

The experts chosen to be members of the GEC committee had mixed skills, in two different senses. On the one hand, the group was made up of people with various sorts of training and technical or scientific specializations. Fourteen experts were members of the GEC committee for all or part of its work. They were four economists, three engineers, three lawyers, three natural scientists and one medical doctor. They had a high level of education, much higher than the average level of all members of the extra-parliamentary committees studied so far (Germann 1981). This certainly contributed to the authority of their report as a technocratic tool for the government as it dealt with such a complex area as energy. On the other hand, the GEC experts were carefully chosen for the social and political trends they represented. The interests of the energy sector were well taken into account: no fewer than five members defended them, of whom three, including the chairman, were supposed to speak mainly for the electricity industry. This heavy representation of the energy sector was appreciated from the start and criticized as making the group unlikely to improve the environment. A few members did not belong to the private sector: they were academics, senior civil servants, one representative of the cantons, and even a woman, who was a member of the Socialist Party (the same party as the Minister for Traffic and Energy); she was also the vice-chair of the committee, with an important symbolic role, but she did not take an active part in the debates. Finally, two representatives of the national organized ecology movements were also members.

CONSENSUS FORMATION IN THE GLOBAL ENERGY CONCEPTION COMMITTEE

Obviously, the group had been composed to reflect some of the conflicts in Swiss society, although the ecologists were in a small minority and were given less weight then they already had in public opinion. This imperfect attempt at balancing the rival views within the committee can be interpreted as a first step towards a consensus. The committee would not split up into equal and antagonistic factions. The ecologists were represented and this allowed the federal government to resist the criticism of being too partial towards the interests of the energy industry. At the same time, the ecologists were so few that they might reasonably expect to be ready to compromise or, at least, not to presume to dominate the outcome. In practice, consensus proved very difficult, as may be seen if we distinguish here the public presentation and reporting of the committee's work from the way in which it actually dealt with the scenarios in its discussions. When the final report was published at the end of 1978, the Swiss mass media all commented upon the 'global conception' of this expert committee as if it had jointly agreed on only one such view. One learned from reading most papers that a group of highly qualified people had agreed upon this rather vague idea. In the future, it was announced, the State should intervene more in energy policy. This impression of the committee's consensus has been reinforced each time the political authorities have since justified or rationalized a decision on the basis of the implied single and consensual recommendation of the experts' group. The high level of the experts' qualifications and, sometimes, a popular confusion of their political affiliations with this technical or more neutral role contributed to the general image of a consensus having been reached. In various mass media interviews, for instance, the chairman of the committee stated that there had been no role conflict between his being a representative of the private sector (actually the nuclear power industry) and his being an expert in 'global energy conceptions'. His argument was that energy producers were the most competent in that field anyway, because of their experience.

Yet a closer look at the committee's work on the four scenarios reveals that the conflict between traditional and new values had not been definitely resolved. The committee reported that the two middle scenarios, (2) and (3), should be adopted as national policy. While the group did agree to move to this central ground, it still showed its division in supporting both of two different options. The report is quite clear: a 'weak majority' favoured scenario (3) (a new constitutional article permitting state intervention) against a 'strong minority' favouring scenario (2) (no such new legal bases). The minority was particularly strong as it included the chairman. The way in which the 'extreme' scenarios were eliminated is also instructive. Scenario (1) (laissez-faire) had been unanimously rejected: all members thought that the *status quo* should not last any longer. Actually, almost everyone in the country agreed on this point; it was precisely the reason why the GEC had been created. But the fourth scenario , calling for State powers to impose 'stability' in energy consumption, had been rejected only after a rather long conflict within the group. Antagonism between the values of the ecological organizations and the industry representatives was clear. Two experts had been appointed to the committee in order to defend ecological views: after a while, one of them left the committee and the other left his position in one of the most important national ecology organizations. A 'stabilization study', which was the basis for scenario (4) had been produced by a group called EWU (Energie – Wachstum – Umwelt: Energy – Growth – Environment). The academic qualifications of the EWU group were as high as those of the GEC committee. After having been rejected by the GEC committee, this study was published by the national ecological organizations a couple of months before the official committee report. It was known then as the 'alternative global conception'.

What conclusion can we draw so far? The support of the GEC experts for scenarios (2) and (3) shows that they were aware of real controversy in society. They did take it into account in their proposals, but only in a weakened version. It appeared that the vitality of new groups and ecological organizations had been somewhat underestimated.

THE COMMITTEE FOR THE REVISION OF THE ATOMIC LAW

The origin of this committee is related to the work of the GEC committee in several ways. It was created one year later (1975) to propose amendments to the law on nuclear energy which had existed since 1959. The opposition to the uncontrolled economic growth and the sensitivity of the citizens to environmental problems seemed to be most visible in the nuclear power field, as if this sector functioned as a magnifying glass. People who did not feel deeply concerned about a 'global energy conception' considered the dangers of radioactivity as a much more concrete fact. The occupation of the nuclear power construction site in Kaiseraugst had made most of the Swiss population aware of the problem. The pressure put on the federal government did not come only from this social disruption. The anti-nuclear opposition also used an established constitutional channel, the popular initiatives. In a few months, the necessary 100,000 valid signatures were collected and the issue of nuclear power turned into a subject of political negotiation. An amendment of the atomic power law of 1959 was clearly demanded.

In the 1950s nuclear energy had been rather welcomed in Switzerland. Although it was a matter of national concern, its production was in fact left pretty much to private industry. Political authorities seemed to have little to say in that field. Members of the Federal Assembly thought they had insufficient information and knowledge on those questions. The Federal Council had delegated the legal authority to grant nuclear power station licences to the Department of Traffic and Energy. The decision was merely administrative and the system was close to a free market, according to the old law; any applicant had a legal claim to the licence, provided he fulfilled some requirements about safety measures. But, at the beginning of the 1970s, popular opinion about nuclear energy had changed: from being a technical matter it turned into a political problem. The result of the popular initiative did not require the country to abandon all future nuclear production but it did make it clear that it should not be left to private industry and that concerned citizens and political authorities should take an active part in the decision-making process. Under the pressure of the popular initiative and of the events in Kaiseraugst, the government had to react quickly. It nominated the RAL committee to attempt a total revision of the atomic law. But, for reasons of urgency, part of the law had to be amended immediately, especially concerning the licence-granting procedure because the decision on Kaiseraugst was at stake. Therefore the experts worked in two steps: they first formulated a federal decree, which was accepted by the Federal Assembly and by popular vote and which became law in 1979; then they drafted a total revision of atomic law to be submitted to the parties and interested groups for consultation.

The RAL committee was very small, with only five members: three university law professors (from the universities of Basle, Berne and Geneva); the Department of Justice's director of its section concerned with jurisdiction – and one retired judge of the supreme Court, who was the chairman of the committee. In addition, civil servants of the Department of Traffic and Energy participated in meetings as advisers. Obviously, this committee was formed in quite a different way from the GEC committee. We might call these law professionals revising the atomic law 'first degree experts'. They are all legal technicians asked to put social changes into the proper juridical form. There were no mixed skills or representative roles as with the GEC committee: interest groups or political trends were not represented. Although the RAL experts might well have had personal sympathies for either traditional or new values on energy issues, they were supposed to function wholly as jurists. Their approach is 'idealistic', in contrast to the 'realpolitik' which characterized the debates of the GEC committee. Detached from the influence of social and political groups and their various options and conflicts, the RAL committee was appointed to propose an improved relationship between the law and value changes in society. The government announcement said that the group had been nominated in order to improve the decision-making process in the nuclear power sector, to make it more transparent and more democratic.

CONSENSUS FORMATION IN THE REVISION OF
THE ATOMIC LAW COMMITTEE

As a consequence of those characteristics, the RAL committee did not reflect the political divisions in civil society. It experienced no conflict such as those that had occured in the GEC committee. There was no reason for conflict since these legal experts had no vested interests in either energy or ecology. They simply used their professional knowledge and skills to try to clarify some aspects of State intervention in the nuclear power sector. This intervention question was not so simple as it seemed. The popular initiative had demanded a transfer of some control of the nuclear industry to political actors. The debate seemed classical: some popular and partisan voices were asking for State protection against and the regulation of private interests, while the nuclear energy industry opposed the idea as being contrary to a valued free market system. But when they closely analysed the situation, the RAL experts noted that the Swiss nuclear plants were not to such a large extent in private hands: most of the shareholders were public or semi-public organizations. One had to admit that the State was already present in the nuclear sector. What then was so innovative or so debatable about the demand? An expert suggested that the argument should not be understood in a strictly legal way but in a political one. After the social unrest concerning the Kaiseraugst plant during the early 1970s, it was generally admitted that some political authority should have decision-making power in granting licences to nuclear plants. The pressure from the popular initiative did not leave any time for philosophical discussions about State intervention *versus* a free market system. It was necessary to define in concrete terms who was to intervene in granting licences, how and when. Interestingly enough, the debate on values was transferred to that level. The question became: will the government or the parliament be the proper authority for that matter?

The RAL experts knew that there was no consensus on the topic. A consultation organized in 1977 and asking for the preferences of the cantons, parties and groups, showed that one of the main arguments in favour of giving the power to the government was based on nuclear power being seen as a purely technical matter. Those who wanted the parliament to decide, thought that, on the contrary, decisions taken in the nuclear field were important and therefore political, and so should be submitted to a democratic process. Most of the ecological organizations supported this latter view as did the Left parties, trade unions, consumer organizations, the youth section of an important Right-wing party and the cantonal executives of Basle, Aargau, Geneva and Ticino. All the other cantons were in favour of the government (the Federal Council) being the main authority and so were most of the Right parties and groups, plus the energy industry. This conflict over whether nuclear power is 'technical' or 'political' did reflect something of the old Right – Left distinction but it also showed some new values. Given this division in society the jurists of RAL proposed a two-headed solution which might have satisfied both sides. The Federal Council was to grant the licence, after having checked a number of safety and other conditions at the national level, and the Federal Assembly would then be asked to ratify this decision.

On the question of the power relationship concerning nuclear power between the Confederation and the cantons significant disagreements also appeared. Curiously, the energy industry, which is traditionally against State intervention, favoured more centralization, on the grounds that nuclear production is of national concern and that local communities and cantons should not interfere in the decision. This is precisely the kind of thinking – political centralization related to big and impenetrable technologies – which is criticized by ecologists and their sympathizers, in most countries. The popular initiative actually asked for all concerned citizens to be able to participate in nuclear power decisions. In addition, one must admit that the federalist tradition in Switzerland helps to make decentralization a popular value. Again, the RAL experts dealt with the problem in two steps. In the initial and supposedly urgent decree, they proposed that the most powers be given to the Federal Council. But in the total revision of the relevant law, important powers for the cantons were explicitly restated, namely land-use planning and waters protection powers. It should be noted, however, that the enacting of the new law was postponed until 1990, partly because it seemed very difficult to find a consensus. The relevant groups and parties have since been consulted on it.

Summarizing the contrasts between these two professional committees, we see that, compared to the whole set of expert committees in Switzerland, the GEC group was medium-sized while the RAL group was very small. 'GEC' was variegated in both its technical training and its political or social representation. It also combined technical and representative roles. The RAL committee was wholly technical and homogeneous in that all members were lawyers. The starting-point was the same for both: a political and social conflict whereby the energy crisis had induced demands for innovation: to transform some private activities into more public ones and to transform a technical field into a political one. This conflict pervaded the GEC group, while the RAL committee remained separated from it. Which group was more innovative or responsive? If we limit the answer to the committee's formal reports it seems to have been the RAL committee. The lawyers reached a consensus, while taking into account various expectations, to propose important concessions to the new ecological interests in society. The fact that this committee was more detached from civil society appears to have given it more freedom to respond in that direction. But, in the long run, things are not so clear because its proposals have not yet received consensus agreement from all groups and parties. The political and philosophical differences in society will probably persist and no expert committee can wish them away.

Aubert, J.F. (1978), *Exposé des institutions politiques de la Suisse à partir de quelques affaires controversées [Review of Swiss Political Institutions on the Basis of some Controversial Issues]* (Lausanne: Payot).

Germann, R. (1981), *Ausserparlamentarischer Kommissionen: Die Milizverwaltung des Bundes [Extra-parliamentary Commissions: The militia administration of the Federal Government]* (Berne: Haupt).

Germann, R. *et al.* (1986), *Experts et commissions de la Confédération [Experts and commissions of the Confederation]* (Lausanne: Presses polytechniques romandes).

Germann, R. and Frutiger, A. (1978), Les experts et la politique [Experts and policy]; *Revue suisse de sociologie*, 4, 2, 99–128.

Gorz, A. (1978), *Ecologie et politique [Ecology and Politics]* (Points politiques) (Paris: Seuil)

Inglehart, R. (1977), *The Silent Revolution: Changing values and political styles among Western Publics* (Princeton, NJ: Princeton University Press).

Kriesi, H.P. (1980), *Entscheidungssturkturen und Entscheidungsprozesse in der Schweizer Politik [Decision Structures and Processes in Swiss politics]* (Frankfurt: Campus).

Linder, W. (1979) Planning als demokratischer Prozess [Planning as a democratic process]; in Linder *et al.* (eds), *Planung in der schweizerischen Demokratie [Planning in the Swiss Democracy]* (Berne: Haupt).

Nelkin, D. (1977), *Technological Decisions and Democracy* (Beverly Hills: Sage).

Nelkin, D. (1979), *Controversy. Politics of technical decisions* (London: Sage) 2nd rev. edn 1984.

Nelkin, D. and Pollack, M. (1981), *The Atom Besieged* (Cambridge, MA: MIT Press).

Schroeren, M. (1977), *Z.B. Kaiseraugst. Der gewaltfreie Widerstand gegen das Atomkraftwerk: vom legalen Protest zum zivilen Ungehörsam [Kaiseraugst: Nonviolent Opposition to Atomic Power: from legal protest to civil disobedience]* (Zurich: Schweizerischer Friedensrat).

Tschaeni, H. (1983), *Wer regiert die Schweiz? [Who Rules Switzerland?]* (Zürich: Orell Füssli).

Five

Controversy and Authority in British Official Scientific Advice on Radiation
The Black Report on Sellafield and Children's Leukaemias

SALLY MACGILL

This chapter, like Wolfgang Rüdig's, starts from the popular perception of 'science' being factual, objective and therefore properly authoritative for public policy-making. The highly controversial question of Britain's child leukaemias and their causal links with nuclear plants (notably the Sellafield – formerly Windscale – nuclear fuel reprocessing factory in Cumbria) is reviewed. The professional views of scientists who worked on the official inquiry into this subject are reported: the conclusion is that the 'pedigree' or scientific quality of any conclusions is quite poor and that the growing philosophical and political science literature which questions the objective authority of some science and technology findings or positions is right to do so.

The child leukaemia issue in Britain entered a new phase in early 1990 when Professor Martin Gardner of the Government-financed Medical Research Council reported that children of workers at Sellafield (and others in radioactive work places) got their leukaemias directly from their fathers' affected sperm and not from either background radioactivity or from chance local clusters of the illness, unrelated to nearby nuclear facilities. How the sperm is affected and how it produces the leukaemia are now to be explored – as are questions such as which type of radioactivity causes which leukaemias. 'The Gardner Report' (described by a nuclear industry spokesman as 'just one man's report of one study') immediately stimulated a debate and further reductions in permitted radiation exposures.

Like most dramatic advances, it drew some of its force from the context of earlier studies. As long ago as 1955, an American study of over 3,700 practising radiologists had shown above-average abnormalities in their children. This statistical finding had been repeated thirty years later in a study by the British Government's Office of Population Censuses and Surveys. Several occupations had been compared and the comparison strongly suggested that female radiologists had produced children with more abnormalities than the general population. One group of conditions (malformed anus and rectum) offered a statistically significant figure. A similarly significant link between fathers' job connection with radiation and spina bifida and affected brains in their children was shown in a study of American men at the Hanford nuclear station in Washington state.

Gardner's study went beyond statistical studies (with their risk of highlighting 'false positives') towards showing the causal link. But the statistical work goes on, including the study reported in March 1991 in the *British Medical Journal* by Dr Cartwright of the University of Leeds showing higher-than-average leukemia rates among the children of several occupational groups of fathers, including those continually exposed to both wood dust and benzine. The incidence was 2–3 times higher in the case of radiation exposure. During 1991, Professor Gardner was engaged in a particular study of congenital damage near to Sellafield. For a review of the issue by a UK Atomic Energy Authority adviser, see Grimston (1991). No doubt another official expert committee will be asked, in due course, to review Gardner's and other similar studies and recommend limits on long-term, low-dose standards.

THE UNCERTAINTY OF SCIENCE

It is useful to take stock at the outset of some of the more obvious factors which undermine the authority of science in the public policy arena. They do not act in isolation from one another but, on the contrary, in a complex symbiosis. The factors include: the tendency of different individuals to have widely differing perceptions of which scientific evidence and argument really is pertinent to a given policy context; the difficulty of representing intangibles scientifically; the tendency for different individuals to have different preferences and value judgments over optimum decision outcomes, even in many cases where there is an agreed body of scientifically-based 'facts'; tendencies towards political domination and manipulation; massive shortfalls in understanding among interest-groups in and participants of the science that is being brought to bear on decision-making – recent studies have commented on the appalling scientific illiteracy of the adult population in general (Royal Society 1985) and its incomprehension of specific matters (as found by Lucas (1987) in the case of radiation hazards, for example). One may reflect on whether the findings of studies on other aspects of adult literacy or knowledge might be any more positive!

Two further factors are considered at greater length in this chapter. The first of these arises where there are questions which may be formulated in conventional scientific terms, but which are beyond the capacity of science to answer definitively: 'trans-scientific' problems, in Weinberg's (1972) terminology. These are cases where there are significant uncertainties in the existing body of scientific knowledge, of a kind which cannot be resolved within the time-frame of decision-making. The second arises out of recognition that it is not sufficient merely to think of science as an (independent) input into public policy: it should be thought just as routinely that public policy is an input into science, both in terms of influencing the multiple agendas of problems which attract scientific research interest and related resources and in terms of the inevitable boundary effects which influence the undertaking, perhaps even the outcome, of that research.

Controversy over the potential association between radiation in the environment and the incidence of leukaemia and other cancers, the chosen context for this chapter, embodies and reflects all the above factors.

RADIATION HAZARDS: UNCERTAINTY

Much controversy stems from gaps and inconclusiveness within what is known about patterns of concentrations of radionuclides in the environment, about their passage through pathways *via* which people might receive critical radiation doses, and about possible detrimental biological effects of different radionuclides in different concentrations in locations in the human body. On each of these aspects there are crucial respects in which the wealth of accumulated knowledge, as with that in all areas in which there is continued scientific research interest, is neither definitive nor complete. The newspaper headline 'Radiation more harmful than previously thought' (*The Independent* 14 November 1987), bearing evocative reflection of the still-evolving state of knowledge, was all the more telling for its source in statements by the National Radiological Protection Board, the UK's statutory advisory body on radiation standards. In this case a reassessment of fatal cancers which followed the atomic bombs at Hiroshima and Nagasaki pointed to a twofold increase over that previously estimated in the assessed risk for the exposed population (NRPB 1987). Risk from natural radiation in the environment has also recently undergone radical reassessment (Hughes *et al.* 1988).

The wider literature displays many instances of crucial uncertainty. Eisenbud (1987), for example, takes stock of uncertainties in models which are used to assess the transmission of radioactivity through environmental pathways. He notes the limited extent to which such models have been validated in the field, or evaluated through statistical studies; the difficulty in assigning credible numerical values to model parameters; the cumulative effect of uncertainties in individual model components and the sometimes complex interactions between components and the omission of crucial parameters from such models. Elsewhere, Searle (1987) comments on the considerable extent of uncertainties connected with assessing genetic risk from exposure to radiation, in spite of extensive research. Others have observed crucial disagreements among experts and the impossibly long time horizons which would be entailed for research necessary to resolve them (Mazur 1973).

In summary, notwithstanding the existence of a robust body of effective scientific knowledge on many aspects of the potentially harmful effects of environmental radioactivity, there are also deficiencies. Any assessment of human health risks must employ or involve such inputs as studies of human subjects in different and dissimilar contexts, inferences from animal data (often laboratory-based) or the interpolation and extrapolation of data.

Alongside uncertainties in knowledge about potentially harmful effects of environmental radioactivity, there exist small but alarming and unexplained clusters of leukaemia and other cancers. In some instances a link with radiation has been established. In others it has not, but neither has it been conclusively rejected (Linet 1985).

THE PROVENANCE OF UNCERTAINTY ABOUT ENVIRONMENTAL RADIATION RISKS

Gaps in knowledge about potentially harmful effects of environmental radioactivity are of varied origin. The 'trans-scientific' nature of much related research has already been referred to. But as with gaps in other subjects, they are also in part bound up with the historical evolution of research priorities. The inevitable limitations on resources available to fund research have forced choice and prioritization as a matter of course. The outcome has evolved from the interrelation between what sponsors (private industry, the military, government departments, official research councils, private benefactors) have wanted to fund and what scientists have wanted to research. It has been, and continues to be, an interrelation between historical inertia, self-interests, chance events, external pressures (such as public outcries or mass media scares) and far-sighted innovative developments.

Quite apart from levels of research support which have been available, research priorities have also been shaped by prevailing institutional structures. It should not be imagined that all potential research is equally viable. Some will be well suited to the prevailing structure of research institutions and their accumulated bodies of expertise; while some will fall between administrative divisions, or require an unrealistic degree of synthesis, co-operation or change from established practices. In the United Kingdom there are many separate institutions with research interests in potentially harmful effects of environmental radioactivity: the National Radiological Protection Board, the Safety and Reliability Directorate of the UK Atomic Energy Authority, the Medical Research Council, the Institute of Terrestrial Ecology, universities, the nuclear industry itself and its regulatory organisations, the military – and there are many internal divisions within these individual institutions. Each has its own interests and biases – in choice of research priorities, mode of research activity, derivation and disclosure of results – and there is no overall co-ordinating authority or central forum for open debate. The consequence is an inevitable degree of inconsistency and fragmentation across the field as a whole: a kind of institutionally-maintained ignorance. Effective peer review, so essential for the validation of research findings, can also be seriously limited.

These points are well illustrated in the recent launching (notwithstanding the existing range of research establishments) of a new designated body in the United Kingdom with significant health representation, to enable more complete review of scientific evidence, and subsequent decisions on action, with regard to the control of permitted radioactive discharges. This is the Committee on Medical Aspects of Radiation in the Environment (COMARE 1986, 1988). There remain grounds to question the balance of expertise represented on this committee, its size and its *modus operandi*.

Further illustration of institutional limitations is seen in those cases where unofficial expertise and special local knowledge which members of the public acquire through their everyday activities (living near or working within nuclear installations, for example) turns out to eclipse the professional science of established institutions in particular respects. The disclosure by a former nuclear industry employee of officially unrecorded aerial discharges from the Windscale (now Sellafield) nuclear fuel reprocessing factory in Cumbria in North West England in the 1950s (COMARE, 1986) was a particularly conspicuous example. The expectation (which proved to be correct) of sheep farmers in West Cumbria that concentrations of radioactivity from Chernobyl fall-out in animal fodder would follow a cyclical pattern while the Government's professional scientists (wrongly) expected that there would be a linear decay is a further instance. Other illustrations are provided from time to time in mass media news reportage. For example, the fact that an area in North and West Yorkshire was subject to relatively high contamination from Chernobyl fall-out was originally missed from the official record due to inadequate co-ordination between different statutory authorities. In other cases, 'institutionally maintained' ignorance is not necessarily exposed.

CASE STUDY: SELLAFIELD AND THE BLACK INQUIRY

A particularly striking case study is that of controversy over discharges of radiation into the environment from the spent nuclear fuel reprocessing operations at Sellafield and the increased incidence of leukaemia among the children of Seascale, the nearest village (Macgill 1987). This was the subject of an urgently commissioned government inquiry following unusually prominent mass media exposure of related issues in the autumn of 1983. To an outside observer, this was a scientific inquiry, conducted under the chairmanship of an eminent medical expert, Sir Douglas Black. It was charged with establishing the evidence surrounding allegations of an association between Sellafield's radiation environment and an increased incidence of leukaemia among children in the vicinity. Its report was published the following summer (Black 1984a).

Three critical numerical measures or quantities emerged from the Black Inquiry. Firstly, a radio-biological estimate of the number of deaths from leukaemia which it was calculated could have been caused by Sellafield discharges (accidental and planned) over the period 1957–1975 was 0.1. Secondly, an epidemiological estimate of the number of cases of leukaemia among the child population of Seascale over the same period was four cases. Thirdly, the factor of disparity between these two numbers is, of course, forty. Reassurance offered by Sir Douglas Black at the conclusion of his inquiry to anyone concerned about a possible health hazard in the vicinity of Sellafield was based on the smallness of the first two numbers and the magnitude of the last. The factor of disparity was, in effect, interpreted as a 'safety factor'.

If the three critical quantities could be taken as hard, robust 'truths', the scientific basis for the reassurance would itself be beyond doubt. As it was, the report of the Black Inquiry included acknowledgement of a number of sources of uncertainty which might undermine the integrity of its key estimates, and subsequent commentators drew attention to further aspects (Crouch 1985, COMARE 1986; Macgill and Funtowicz 1988). The uncertainties surrounding the first of these three quantities – the 0.1 deaths from leukaemia – will be given specific consideration here, by way of illustration.

The Black Inquiry explicitly recognized five sources of uncertainty potentially undermining the integrity of 0.1 as a worst case estimate of the number of leukaemia deaths that could be attributable to radiation discharges from Sellafield (Black 1984a, paras 4.5 and 4.85). These were: (i) undetected discharges that may have given rise to additional radiation doses to the public; (ii) possible underestimating of ingestion, inhalation and absorption into the body of certain radionuclides; (iii) inaccurate estimating of gut transfer factors for some radionuclides; (iv) inaccuracies in the model used to calculate the dose to the red bone marrow; (v) the possibility that the Seascale area has an unusual concentration of unusually susceptible children. This was clear, though not necessarily conscious, acknowledgement by the Black Committee of its being faced with a very different sort of field of inquiry from that of a laboratory science, where measurements can be made in detail and with precision, models can be extensively tested and properly calibrated and boundary conditions can be specified under the control of the investigator. It was instead a case of making the best of imperfect measurements or untested models and of drawing plausible inferences about environmental conditions, alongside some more robust elements of knowledge on particular aspects.

The above five sources of uncertainties led the Black Committee to qualify the public reassurance which it might otherwise have found it possible to give having established such a small number of attributable leukaemia deaths (only 0.1). Recommendations for further research to remedy some of the acknowledged gaps in knowledge were included in the committee's report.

A heated 'scientific' debate followed the publication of the Black Report (notably in *Nature, New Scientist, The Guardian* and the *British Medical Journal*; see Crouch 1985 for a review). Contributors drew attention to sources of imperfection and uncertainty surrounding the estimate of 0.1 beyond those which were explicitly acknowledged in the Report itself. Sir Douglas's concluding qualified reassurance was consequently perhaps not as heavily qualified as it should have been.

That the Black Inquiry failed to take account of significant unreported aerial discharges was most dramatically revealed in February, 1986 when a former Sellafield employee stated that some of a quantity of 20-30 kilograms of uranium (as compared to the only 400 grams previously recorded and incorporated into the Black Report's calculations) had been discharged from Sellafield into the atmosphere between 1952 and 1955. Although inclusion of this additional amount of uranium in a revised calculation does not appreciably affect the end result of 0.1 attributable cases of leukaemia, it has been widely interpreted as showing the incompleteness of the original calculation. Indeed, more recently, the official advisory committee established as a result of one of the Black Report's own recommendations (the Committee on Medical Aspects of Radiation in the Environment) has remarked:

> The way in which these data (the additional uranium) came to light is unsatisfactory and undermines our confidence in the adequacy and completeness of available data ... we have to stress that we cannot exclude the possibility that other significant releases from the [Sellafield] plant could have occurred and not been detected.

There is also a possibility of more significant marine discharges than those recognised in the Black Report. A serious beach contamination incident in November 1983 eventually became common knowledge (Walker and Macgill 1988). What is also significant to observe is the detection, during laboratory analysis of beach debris following that incident, of contaminated articles on the shoreline which could not be dated to November 1983 (Woodhead, Jeffries and Barker 1985). These articles are a further potential indicator of radiation discharges from Sellafield which were not accounted for by the Black Committee.

Others have criticized what they consider to be an undue degree of averaging in some of the key calculations underlying the Black Report. They suspect that this has led to an understatement of several potentially crucial factors. These include the possible generation of hot particles through chemical binding of actinides (radioactive metals) to particles of sediment; large variations of radioactivity found in plants, animals and soils; and resuspension of contaminated sediments in seaspray. Further doubts have been raised about whether sufficient acknowledgement was made of the wide diversity of physiological and biochemical characteristics of different people, and their different sensitivities to cancer induction by radiation, due to factors such as age, viral infections, immunological deficiencies and even nutrition. These were noted in addition to more general scientific uncertainties in knowledge about the metabolism and biological effects of radionuclides in animals, let alone in adult or young human beings.

Other sources of criticism about the truth of the 0.1 estimate have focused on the possibility of unacknowledged environmental pathways through which children may have been inadvertently contaminated. In any complex environmental study, it is impossible to guarantee the comprehensive identification of all critical interconnections. 'Hidden' pathways from Sellafield might arise from contaminated objects being taken off-site by Sellafield employees (either inadvertently or deliberately for their perceived use or sale value) or from workers in the radioactive areas being insufficiently decontaminated (either due to inconvenience, pressure of time or lack of awareness) and going home with contamination in their hair, fingernails or clothing.

It is not the place here to seek to make some final judgment on the quality of the above criticisms and their significance for the radiobiological estimate of 0.1. While some commentators have made them with force and even vehemence, they have been dismissed by others as irrelevant, or, at most, only marginally significant. A more philosophical appraisal of the 'pedigree' of the 0.1 estimate can, however, usefully be made.

The estimate of 0.1 was derived from radiobiological studies involving three key stages in the path which the contaminants may take. Stage One of the studies covers reported discharges from the Sellafield installation; routine monitoring data; and models of the transmission and transformation of radiation through the environment. Stage Two is the uptake of radionuclide contamination from the environment which constitutes doses received by young people in the local area. Stage Three consists of models of the pathogenic effects of these estimated doses. Table 1 offers a framework or matrix for assessing the robustness of knowledge derived for each of these stages.

Figure 5.1 The 'pedigree' matrix of data inputs, theories and acceptability of radiobiological studies

Data input	Theoretical structures	Peer review and acceptance	Colleague consensus	Score (code)
experimental data	established theory	total	all but cranks	4
historic or field data	theoretically based model	high	all but rebels	3
calculated data	computational models	medium	competing schools	2
educated guess	statistical processing	low	embryonic field	1
uneducated guess	working definitions	none	no opinion	0

In terms of this framework or matrix, the strength of quantitative estimates will depend on the strength of the theoretical, empirical and sociological components of related research. The theoretical component ranges from established theory (at best) to working definitions (at worst). The empirical component covers experimental data (at best) to uneducated guesses (at worst). The other two criteria for evaluating the estimates' strength are peer review and acceptance and the mature character of the field as a whole (colleague consensus). An account of the origin of this framework can be found in Funtowicz and Ravetz (1987).

Figure 5.2: Estimates of radiation exposure from nuclear installation discharges: practitioners' views of their basis and reliability

CRITERIA	Data input	Theoretical development	Peer review and acceptance	Colleague consensus
Stage One	1–3	3	2–3	3
Stage Two	1–3	3	2–3	2
Stage Three	1–3	1–2	1–2	1–2

A score can be assigned to Stages One, Two and Three for each of the four criteria in Figure 5.1. These scores derive from the terms in which scientists involved with related research for the Black Inquiry themselves spoke about these matters in subsequent interviews (see Macgill and Funtowicz 1988). The scores could run from zero (low or worst) to 4 (high or best).

Taking Stage One first, 'data input' was regarded by these scientists as of variable quality: it was partly historical field data, partly interpolation between measurements, and partly educated guesswork (scores of 1–3 were given for 'data input' (as is shown in Table 5.2)). Still on Stage One, the processes whereby radionuclides in the discharges may pass through various pathways in the environment were described by the scientists as being understood in broad theoretical terms; theoretically-based models were used to depict these processes, yielding a score of 3 on the second criterion in Figure 5.2 ('theoretical development'). The degree of peer acceptance of the estimate was regarded as 'medium to high' (scoring 2–3) with this acceptance seen as disputed only by rebels (score 3).

Overall, the string of resulting scores (Figure 5.2, line 1) depicts a weighted qualification about the possible integrity of the estimation process; its data input aspect being particularly weak. Overall, it conveys a picture neither of total confidence in understanding, nor of complete ignorance about the underlying phenomena of interest in Stage One.

For Stage Two (estimation of the uptake of possible radionuclide contamination from the environment to various sites in the human body) the 'data input' criterion was also described by the scientists as being a mix of field (monitor) data, interpolation between measurements and more or less educated (someone suggested uneducated) guesswork: (scores of 1–3). The estimation itself was, again, also said to be derived from theoretically-based models (a score of 3). The epistemological development of the field itself (colleague consensus) was regarded as being more questionable than for Stage One, with competing theories in play on a number of crucial aspects (thus scoring only 2). The peer acceptance of the result was regarded as being 'medium to high' (score 2–3). Overall the assessment (see Figure 5.2, line 2) depicts a somewhat more heavily qualified result than for Stage One, given the weaker perception of an expert consensus about the state of maturity of the field.

Stage Three (estimating the pathogenic effects of the estimated radiation doses) was generally regarded as being a less secure process than those of the previous two stages. Knowledge in this field has been significantly developed in animal laboratory work and in military contexts, but great problems were seen by the respondents in producing reliable estimates for human beings or for low-level discharges. Still greater problems were perceived for a specific cancer in the case of children. The 'data input' criterion was said to comprise some field data and some educated guesswork, or worse (score 1–3). On the 'theoretical development' criterion the modes in Figure 5.1 of 'computational models' and 'statistical processing' were deemed the most fitting categories (scores 1–2). The peer review and acceptance criterion was described as 'medium to low' (a score of 1–2); and there was a view among some interviewees that the 'colleague consensus' is characterised by 'competing schools' while others felt that it is as yet embryonic (score 1–2). Overall, the derived codings here (Figure5.2, line 3) depict a marked weakness in this stage of the overall estimation process.

All in all, the contrast in the derived 'pedigree' or 'quality assessment' codings for each of the three different stages reflects the differing levels of understanding of the processes which constitute each stage. This, in turn, brings out crucial differences in the degree of qualification which should be associated with any corresponding quantitative estimates. The contrast is more striking if we follow the convention of choosing the weakest of possible alternative scorings for any given mode and criteria. This then gives for Stage One (1,3,2,3); for Stage Two (1,3,2,2) and for Stage Three (1,1,1,1).

The overall implication of these derived scores (the formal maximum is, of course, 4,4,4,4) is that the 'true' estimate of radiation-induced health risk as a result of Sellafield's discharges may not be 0.1 deaths over the given period (contrary to initial impressions). There could be a high degree of confidence that this was the 'true' number only if the resulting 'pedigree codings' were higher. At the same time, the low scorings, particularly for the last of the three stages, means that it is not possible to derive any other estimate than 0.1; the 'true' figure for attributable deaths may be much lower, or indeed, much higher.

Within the domain of 'science' the appearance of relatively low quality assessment scorings should be the occasion for neither shame nor concealment. It is merely a true reflection of the quality of what can be or has been produced in the face of irremediable difficulties, uncertainties or gaps in scientific knowledge and within the limits of the time-scale of and resource inputs to the studies from which the estimate was produced. Within the policy arena, however, ramifications of 'low pedigree' codings may be considerably more problematic.

PUBLIC POLICY AS AN INPUT TO SCIENCE

Can the criticisms of the 'pedigree' of radiobiological studies be used to support any suggestion (or hypothesis) that Black's reassurance was wholly unjustified – or that radioactive discharges from Sellafield were indeed the likely cause of the leukaemia in the children of Seascale? It would first be necessary to undertake a corresponding assessment of uncertainties in evidence about other possible causes – viruses, environmental factors, hereditary factors and so on. After all, although radiation is the only currently known cause of leukaemia in children, most actual cases of the disease have an unknown cause. After decades of research, the aetiology of leukaemia in children remains largely unknown.

The Black Inquiry is a striking example of how scientific inquiry almost inevitably becomes bound up with and shaped by particular political and social uses. There were several senses in which public policy in effect became an input to the ostensibly solely scientific Black Inquiry. Most obviously, the initiation of the inquiry was due to the mass media bringing the Sellafield controversy into wide public view; the Government's political response was to commission an inquiry.

The inquiry was a mechanism for 'answering' public calls for 'action'. Almost as obviously, there was a strong policy constraint on what could be published as the conclusion of the inquiry. The credibility of the nuclear industry and of its regulatory agencies would be bound up with Black's conclusions. This involves major industrial and political investments, laying a very heavy responsibility indeed on any report which would, even by implication, accuse the officially regulated nuclear industry of having caused the deaths of children in its vicinity. Beyond these rather obvious points on the creation and conclusion of the Black Inquiry, policy input can be identified in a number of other ways. Indeed, it conditioned, most substantially, the inquiry's whole focus of interest.

The Inquiry's concentration on radiation from Sellafield as the possible cause of leukaemia in Seascale children (as distinct from other possible causes) was determined not so much from 'objective' scientific considerations, as from the dramatic and highly sensitive political context in which the inquiry was originally commissioned: public pressure to accuse or exonerate Sellafield following widely publicized criticism (in a television documentary). Political and social questions of blame were at least as prominent as scientific questions of cause. This blurring of the social with the scientific was most evident in the terms in which Sir Douglas Black (1984b) himself spoke about his inquiry as having concerned 'the case against Windscale'.

A more 'balanced' scientific analysis and, on some views, a more sensible allocation of scarce resources for research might have been to give systematic consideration to the weight of evidence for all hypothesized causes of leukaemia among Seascale children. This would have opened the way for both the inquiry itself and its outcome to have had a very different complexion. As it was, other possible causes of leukaemia in Seascale children were virtually excluded from consideration.

The narrowness of Black's focus has been more widely recognized in recent times. There is now more evident consideration of other possible causes of the leukaemia in Seascale children (though lacking the former political urgency) and more wide-ranging research studies. There is also more widespread acknowledgement of the impossibility of resolving the Sellafield controversy without reference to other nuclear establishments. Finally, there is more widespread acknowledgement that the 'science' that needs to be brought to bear in relation to all these matters is less conclusive than had been thought at the time of the Black Inquiry (*The Independent*, 19 November 1987).

Black, (Sir) D. (1984a), *Investigation of Possible Increased Incidence of Cancer in West Cumbria* (London: HMSO).
Black, (Sir) D. (1984b), *An Anthology of False Antitheses* (London: Nuffield Provincial Hospital Trust).
Committee on Medical Aspects of Radiation in the Environment (1986), *First Report* (London: HMSO).

Committee on Medical Aspects of Radiation in the Environment (1988), *Second Report*
   (London: HMSO).
Crouch, D. (1985), Science, teleology and society: child cancer around the Sellafield
   nuclear reprocessing plant; MSc Dissertation, University of Sussex, SPRU.
Eisenbud, E. (1987), *Environmental Radioactivity* (New York: Academic Press), 3rd edn.
Funtowicz, S.O. and Ravetz, J.R. (1987), Qualified quantities – towards an arithmetic of
   real experience; in Forge, J. (ed.) *Measurement, Realism and Objectivity*
   (Dordrecht: D. Reidel).
Grimston, M. (1991), Leukemia's alleged links with nuclear power establishments; *Atom,*
   409, January, 6–10.
Hughes, J.S. *et al.* (1988), *Radiation Exposure of the UK Population – 1988 review* .
   NRPB R227 (London: HMSO).
The Independent (1987), 19 November, 2.
Linet, M.S. (1985), *The Leukaemias: Epidemiologic aspects* (Oxford: Oxford University
   Press).
Lucas, A.M. (1987), Public knowledge of radiation; *Biologist,* 34, 125–9.
Macgill, S.M. (1987), *The Politics of Anxiety: Sellafield's cancer-link controversy*
   (London: Pion).
Macgill, S.M. and Funtowicz, S.O. (1988), The 'pedigree' of radiation estimates: an
   exploratory analysis in the context of exposure of young people in Seascale as a result
   of Sellafield discharges; *Journal of Radiological Protection,* 8,2, 77–86.
Mazur, A. (1973), Disputes between experts; *Minerva,* 11, 243–63.
National Radiological Protection Board (1987), *Interim Guidance on the Implications of
   Recent Revisions of Risk Estimates and the ICRP 1987 Como Statement*, NRPB-GS9
   (London: HMSO).
The Royal Society (1985), *The Public Understanding of Science*
   (London: The Royal Society).
Searle, A.G. (1987), Genetic hazards of radiation; *Biologist,* 34, 153–6.
Walker, G.P. and Macgill, S.M. (1988), Communicating risk: news media reportage of a
   significant nuclear contamination incident in the UK; University of Leeds School of
   Geography, WP 501.
Weinberg, A.M. (1972), Science and trans-science; *Minerva,* 10, 209–22.
Woodhead, D.S., Jeffries, D.F. and Barker, C.J. (1985), Contamination of beach debris
   following an incident at BNF plc; *Journal of Radiological Protection,* 5, 21–32.

Six

Advice, Legitimacy and Nuclear Safety in Britain

MICHAEL SAWARD

This particular chapter within the group contained in this volume which concern nuclear power ties together the public or social requirements which affect the expert adviser or regulator in a scientific field and the technical requirements demanded by the adviser's or regulator's professional community. The public seek reassurance on the safety and general public value of an impenetrable and disturbing technology. Professional peers seek clarity and accuracy in these technical requirements but may also support some derogation of them in the interests of commercial operation.

Michael Saward's commentary on the British nuclear power industry and its public credibility on the safety question reviews the remarkable rise of the British type of major public inquiry as the main current vehicle for determining the public legitimacy of nuclear power. He describes the growing public authority of the Nuclear Installations Inspectorate and predicts its further development as the public's (as well as the Government's) adviser and innovator on the safe operation of nuclear generating, fuel reprocessing and other plants – particularly if the recent crisis of commercial confidence in the industry's economics does not, after all, postpone new nuclear stations indefinitely.

This chapter reminds us that the subject of expert advice to governments, on scientific issues at least, must include the vital aspect of expert advice to society itself. It shows how the balance between these two objectives has changed in the case of British nuclear power during the last twenty years and may continue to change.

INTRODUCTION

What does it take to render credible the case that nuclear installations are sufficiently 'safe'? One non-answer is 'different sets of things at different times'. Major and minor changes in the political, social, economic, scientific and technological context of nuclear power policy have affected the type and source of advice which may be adequate to the task. The aim of this chapter is, firstly, to chart some of the more important changes in source and content of safety advice in the history of the British civil nuclear programme and, secondly, to shed some light on the dilemmas of the technical adviser. It argues that the changes in question must be seen against the shifting background of what has been seen to be adequate to 'legitimize' the safety case.

The thrust of the argument is this. The burden of legitimizing the safety case in Britain has, over the past thirty years, shifted from the UK Atomic Energy Authority (AEA) to the major public inquiries (Windscale, Sizewell and Hinkley Point) and is shifting to the regulatory watchdogs, especially the Health and Safety Executive's (HSE) Nuclear Installations Inspectorate (NII). A broadening of the nuclear 'agenda' has accompanied these shifts, meaning that it has become progressively harder for the relevant advisory authorities to present a convincing safety case. We first address some of the key concepts involved – advice, agenda and legitimacy – and then move on to discuss the AEA, public inquiries and the NII. Finally, we examine the nature and the extent of the burden now being placed on the NII, as the new Government-owned Nuclear Electric PLC strives to sustain political life in British nuclear power.

Like a range of other issues operating on the blurred line between technical and political judgment, the dangers arising from nuclear generation involve a variety of disparate topics. These notably include the dilemmas facing experts in politics, the limits to obtaining independent advice on scientific and technological questions and, more generally, the relationship between 'facts' and 'values'. Not all such issues can be addressed here in their own right; at this more abstract level, we focus on central notions affecting the source and content of safety advice.

ADVICE

People make history, but not in circumstances of their own choosing. Likewise, governments can solicit advice but there are constraints limiting the potential sources and content of advice if it is to perform its legitimizing function. On nuclear safety and other scientific and technological risks, there is a base level where a government must satisfy itself (and must be seen to be so satisfied) that, for example, the chances of a damaging release of radioactivity or a major nuclear accident are low. This base level concerns the fundamental political credibility of particular governments and therefore touches on their very political survival.

Above this baseline lies a significant grey area. In broadly democratic systems, governments must to some minimal degree satisfy also 'public opinion' and certain other actors in the relevant 'policy network'. On issues which are both technically complex and politically or morally contentious, where little grasp of (or even interest in) the strictly technical questions involved can be presumed in the general public, governments need first and foremost credible expert testimony. This is a necessary, though mostly not a sufficient, condition for public credibility.

What a government requires of its experts if (as generally has been the case with the British civil nuclear programme) it has a strong commitment to the use of the technology is advice which combines elements of apparently disinterested expert assessment of how to control or reduce risk and at least implied support for the government policy in question. The risk assessment is needed to satisfy the 'baseline' criteria; the support is needed to bolster the legitimacy of government action in the eyes of 'the public' – as will be discussed below.

Which groups of experts (or anyone else) may sufficiently combine both elements at a given time is not something wholly beyond government influence. At the extremes, governments can mandate advice by creating a source or (on the other hand) can be constrained by factors beyond their control to accept, acknowledge or act upon advice from alternative or even renegade sources (Massey 1988).

Formally, advice to ministers on nuclear safety in Britain comes from the Advisory Committee on the Safety of Nuclear Installations now under the Health and Safety Commission which is, in turn, the governing body of the HSE. In more important informal terms, the Advisory Committee is a highly marginal body: the activities and the opinions of the NII within the HSE carry far more weight with policy-makers, though it does not advise the government in the formal sense as a statutory advisory body.

In principle, the greater the scope for a government to choose which out of a number of credible sources of advice on nuclear safety it will listen to, the greater are the chances of getting the advice it wants which will adequately combine both the elements required: risk assessment and policy support. What decides the scope for government choice in this respect is expert unity or consensus. If it exists (so that, for example, scientists and engineers are in broad agreement about risk levels posed by nuclear installations) the government's scope for choice is minimised; if it does not, government has in principle greater scope to choose between alternative sources of advice, or to play off one source against another.

AGENDA

This, however, does not take us very far. For one thing, it assumes that there is a constant depth, sophistication and credibility of technical advice that would be necessary for policy legitimation at different times. This is a patently false assumption with regard to nuclear safety. Particularly from the mid-1970s, advice on nuclear safety has had to increase its sophistication and credibility to remain adequate to government needs. This was a prime factor in the pressing need for new, more credible, sources of safety advice at the time. External factors had upset the more or less closed relationship between government and its approved advisers. These factors included a worsening economic climate in general and a fall in energy demand in particular; the greater public availability of information on the dangers of nuclear power; and the poor performance of both authorities and reactors in Britain up to that point (Hall 1986 131–48; Patterson 1985). The nuclear agenda was broadening. Greater knowledge about things nuclear accompanied and reinforced a rising tide of criticism of government nuclear policies and key bodies within the industry. At the same time expert unity or consensus, which had operated in favour of nuclear programmemes in Britain, the United States, West Germany and elsewhere, began to break down. As suggested, this gave the government greater scope to choose which experts in a fragmented community of relevant expertise should act as its advisers on safety. However, the emergence of an agenda less favourable to continued nuclear expansion could not, in government eyes, be adequately compensated by the potentially greater choice of sources of advice which it presented. Although in principle the broadening agenda widened government choice, the expert disunity accompanying the change brought new problems. Firstly, it undermined the capacity of successive governments to reassert control over the agenda; secondly, it heightened the possibility that the government's chosen source would have its credibility (and therefore its capacity to legitimize policy) undermined; and, thirdly, it greatly increased the demands which government needed to make of its preferred source of advice.

In sum, for a pro-nuclear power government, the agenda at a given time will ideally be such that its preferred source of safety advice can deliver the goods in the face of expert dissent and wider public scepticism. The emergence of a more volatile and awkward agenda, however, despite granting wider choice to government, places greater demands on the chosen advisers than those faced by earlier advisers if the safety case is to have sufficient credibility and legitimacy.

LEGITIMACY

The relevant agenda is partly made up of received wisdom and knowledge and is to some degree manipulable by well-placed politicians, administrators, experts and dissenters. It carries at a given time implicit (though sometimes rapidly changing) criteria of legitimacy. It carries yardsticks affecting what kind of advice on safety will be adequate to the task of rendering the overall safety case credible. One part of the implicit criteria will relate to the source of safety advice that will best suit government in the circumstances. (Of course, successfully arguing the safety case is only one aspect of the legitimation of nuclear power; legitimation in terms of, for example, economic advantage is dealt with here only in passing.)

'Legitimacy' is, therefore, equated with credibility. That it should be so is far from self-evident; indeed, this should be seen as a stipulative definition of the term. It is helpful to distinguish between 'perceived' and 'moral' legitimacy. Perceived legitimacy refers to subjective assessments of whether a policy, action or non-action is legitimate. Each person or group may use different criteria, consciously or otherwise, in making such assessments. Hence, a given policy or action will be seen as legitimate by some and illegitimate by others. At this level of subjective perception, legitimacy is a wholly relative affair; in principle, no one set of criteria is superior to another. Moral legitimacy, on the other hand, is a more objective measure. At least, it requires a generalizable set of criteria by which to assess the 'moral worth' of policies or actions. Whether an objective set exists (or is discoverable) or whether moral norms can be distilled from a certain time and political culture and used as yardsticks is a huge issue and is not directly relevant here. The point is that in this chapter legitimacy is referred to only as perceived legitimacy.

Within the 'perceived legitimacy' category we can further distinguish two levels of analysis, corresponding broadly with the 'baseline' and 'grey area' noted above. The first is the cruder level of the public opinion poll as the measure of legitimacy; the second involves a minimally necessary degree of, at least, public acquiescence and, at most, public 'consent' to government policy. It is this second sense, encompassing its public credibility, which is the focus of government concern and also the central theme of this chapter.

This is not to say that, for example, opinion poll data and appeals to higher moral norms play no substantive part in influencing government action. But there are other (and shifting) criteria by which governments need to gauge the credibility of their actions. In short, governments need to maintain a broad societal perception that their actions are minimally legitimate.

Within this there may, for instance, be a good deal of popular scepticism about nuclear safety but, kept at a certain level, it need not pose a challenge to the 'minimal legitimacy' of government nuclear policy. It is not so much broad public opinion, but rather sufficient expert and media support for government policy, which make up this particular view of legitimacy. From case to case, which of these factors (including measures of public opinion) are more important can and does vary widely. Thus, this chapter does not address issues stemming from the questions of whether the nuclear safety case being argued really is legitimate in some fuller and objective sense of the word. Rather it is the government's effort to maintain a general perception of legitimacy (and changes in that effort which this might require) which is the focus.

Two further points should be kept in mind. Firstly, what can count as legitimate in this sense is conditioned by the policy agenda, that is, both the broader political circumstances and particular developments pertaining to the policy field in question. Secondly, the question of what can count as legitimate will condition which sources of technical advice on policy matters may be able to meet the legitimation demands which flow from a given policy agenda.

It is worth noting that political actors remake the agenda as they respond to it, though the remaking may carry with it unforeseen and unintended consequences. Also, the agenda is not in any sense neutral between actors or outcomes. In itself it is a bearer of power relations: some actors can influence the shape of the agenda more than others can; some will be held more responsible than others for its shape; and some can benefit from it more than others.

BRITISH NUCLEAR SAFETY: THE EARLY YEARS

The AEA in the late 1980s became a shadow of its former self. From being the single dominant force on the civil nuclear scene up to the early 1970s, it became by early 1990 a much-trimmed and politically marginal body, attempting the uphill task of building a commercial role for the fast breeder reactor and generally adapting to the cold climate of a privatized and commercially-led electricity industry in England and Wales.

Before it was progressively broken up and its role changed, the AEA was once the sole source of advice on civil nuclear safety and economics from the time of its creation in 1954. Most of its civil role in the early years was taken up with reactor design and experiments, while the nuclear programmeme as a whole still reflected its military roots (see Gowing 1974 167–238; Valentine 1985 1–26). Concerns about security and secrecy (notably the safeguarding of plutonium stocks), along with the prestige accorded to nuclear physicists and engineers largely flowing from the technical successes of the military nuclear effort, made the fledgling post-war civil nuclear program a natural candidate for a single, centralized public body (Gowing 1974 50). The AEA was the promotor, regulator and adviser to government on all aspects of the program. Its autonomy was rare among public bodies in Britain. As Valentine comments:

> For fifteen years (the AEA) grew formidably in size and power as it maintained control over civil and military projects that were both expanding. The first atomic activity that it did not directly control was the building and operation of the civil power stations, but it provided the design, and the fuel and reprocessing services were supplied from the factories and laboratories established to provide the same services for the military reactors. (Valentine 1985, 23)

Parliament played little role in scrutinizing the Authority's activities. Its voting of funds for the Authority was invariably accompanied by little debate or comment. The tenor of the pre-AEA nuclear program, where the exceptionally high level of secrecy and lack of outside monitoring was a product of 'awe and fear', was little changed (Gowing 1974 56; Hall 1986 44–58). Ministerial responsibility for the programmeme has shifted seven times since 1953 (UKAEA 1984 63), indicating its non-partisan, technical and marginal character in official eyes, at least until more recent years.

The AEA's Health and Safety Branch was formed in 1959. It was intended to be independent of the organization's engineering and nuclear fuels activities (UKAEA 1984, 23). Its creation was mostly due to the recommendations from the Fleck Committees of the previous year, after their inquiries into the fire in 1957 at Windscale (now re-named Sellafield) which remains today as one of the world's most serious releases of radiation. The reports of several committees of inquiry chaired by Sir Alexander (later Lord) Fleck are today strongly discredited in parts, following the official release of internal official papers about the fire in January 1989 under the British 'Thirty Year Rule'. They did not criticize the AEA over the accident, but concluded that too many Government Departments were involved in various aspects of nuclear health and safety (Fleck 1958). The Government's level of trust in the competence of the Authority on safety matters was unshaken. It was not so much a matter of the AEA advising the Government on nuclear safety and always having its expertise on these matters unquestioningly accepted; rather, the trust in its expertise extended to being left alone to be judge and jury as to what was to be accepted as 'safe'. Technical understanding of what might be safe (or 'safe enough') was, of course, limited compared to today.

The perceived national prestige and political or strategic importance of the Authority's work rubbed off on the organization itself. A high level of scientific consensus on nuclear safety coalesced around it. Successive governments were prepared to leave such matters to the AEA's acknowledged expertise. As David Price, MP put it in the House of Commons in February 1959, nuclear safety issues were 'something which to most of us represents a remote and rather obscure sphere of learning' (*Hansard* 1959 882). This in turn encouraged and reinforced an apparent lack of knowledge of, or interest in, the Authority's work on the part of the press and the general public. As Blowers and Pepper comment, the industry's broad legitimacy in the years of the AEA's dominance was implicitly underpinned by the 'passivity and indifference of the mass of the population' (1987 18).

Post-war governments of both parties set an agenda for rapid nuclear development. The initial purpose was to provide the infrastructure and materials for making bombs, but the use of nuclear power for generating the public electricity supply became increasingly important. The advisory machinery on nuclear safety complemented the broader ideology surrounding nuclear development. Legitimation of the safety case was, in effect, achieved by default. Most argument centred on the economic feasibility of commercial reactors compared to coal-fired plants (Hall 1986 50ff.). The capacity of the AEA to legitimize the safety case was not dented by the Windscale fire in 1957 and did not depend on the dissemination, or even the existence, of explicit safety criteria for the design and operation of nuclear plants. The Churchill Government had mandated the AEA as its safety adviser; until the early 1970s the lack of choice as to source of advice was a source of comfort for successive governments.

THE STAKES INCREASE

In broad terms, the 1970s saw some opening up of the civil nuclear program to public debate. The period 1974–78 saw the emergence of local dissent over nuclear waste disposal and issues of siting reactors. Emergent organized dissent focused in particular on the fast breeder reactor (FBR) which was claimed to be a source of virtually limitless cheap energy (Patterson 1985 141–78) and the reprocessing of nuclear fuel rods (Williams 1980, 261-3). The American-based pressure group Friends of the Earth (FoE) was the most prominent of the new dissenters on nuclear power (Williams 1980 261–2; Lowe and Goyder 1983 124ff.). Heightened public attention was facilitated by the report of the Royal Commission on Environmental Pollution, *Nuclear Power and the Environment* (the 'Flowers Report'), in 1976. The Commission's chairman, Sir Brian (now Lord) Flowers, FRS, and his colleagues were critical of the lack of attention given to the problem of what to do with nuclear waste, and of aspects of the planned FBR program.

The AEA came under considerable pressure. Emergent criticism pointed to the links between its civil and military roles, its conflict of interest as both promoter and regulator of the nuclear program and the extraordinary degree of autonomy from parliamentary and public scrutiny it had achieved.

A number of structural changes in the industry fragmented the AEA's responsibilities in order to deal with these and other problems. British Nuclear Fuels Ltd (BNFL) was formed in 1971 out of the AEA's Production Group, partly to bring about a visible separation of aspects of the civil and military programmemes (Valentine 1985 24) and partly to exploit the commercial potential of a separate nuclear fuels organization (Massey 1986, 1988). On matters of safety the National Radiological Protection Board (NRPB) was established in 1970 to take over the task of setting standards for doses of radiation to the public and workers in the industry from the AEA's Health and Safety Branch. Sole responsibility for monitoring the safety of its own nuclear installations, however, remained with the AEA's Safety and Reliability Directorate (UKAEA 1984 43) although some of the facilities transferred to BNFL did come under the inspection of the NII (notably the plutonium-producing reactors and fuel-reprocessing facilities at Windscale). Commercial reactors were owned and run by the former Central Electricity Generating Board (CEGB) and the South of Scotland Electricity Board (SSEB) as the state-owned monopoly generators and were operated under safety licences from the NII. The NII could and did inspect AEA sites from time to time but did not formally license or monitor them. The CEGB and SSEB were always directly responsible in law for the safe operation of their facilities, as are their state-owned successor bodies, Nuclear Electric PLC and Scottish Nuclear PLC.

The agenda had broadened to encompass more organized public scepticism about nuclear safety. As we have noted, some fragmentation of sources of advice to government on safety had occurred but the effect of this was limited. The hiving-off of the AEA's responsibilities did not appear adequate to meeting the legitimation demands of the new climate. There were two paths that could be taken to make up the deficit. Firstly, the AEA, BNFL, the NRPB and the NII, prodded and facilitated by the government, could be more explicit about their safety criteria used in the design and operation of nuclear facilities. If, as they regularly protested, fears about the dangers posed were unwarranted, they could provide the technical information demonstrating this in a form accessible to the non-expert. Secondly, this approach might be avoided if the credibility of the AEA and BNFL, along with the safety regulators, could be restored to something like the level previously enjoyed by the Authority. In essence, this approach would involve some form of genuinely independent and non-governmental confirmation of these bodies' competence, expertise and objectivity, in order to show that they deserved public trust in a field of activity which carried inherent risks.

Of these two paths, the 'justificatory' and the 'confirmatory', the latter was the one followed in the late 1970s and early 1980s. However, as the agenda continued to broaden into the 1980s, more openness and more justification also became evident as the critical pressures on the industry in general intensified.

The task of the confirmation of the relevant authorities fell to the big public inquiry: the Windscale (now Sellafield) inquiry into BNFL's proposed thermal oxide reprocessing plant (THORP) in 1977, the Sizewell 'B' inquiry into the first of the CEGB's proposed family of pressurized water reactors (PWRs) in 1983–5, and the Hinkley Point 'C' inquiry into the second proposed PWR in 1988–9. Issues of safety have figured prominently on each occasion.

It does not require a conspiracy theory to interpret the Parker Report (1978) from the Windscale inquiry as a 'confirming' document. In British nuclear history it is one of the clearest examples of this strategy. The Windscale inspector, Mr Justice Parker (then a High Court judge), displayed in his report and recommendations a notable depth of trust in BNFL and the key regulatory bodies, the NRPB, the NII and the International Commission for Radiological Protection (ICRP), which is the international standard-setting body with respect to radiation doses. Confirmation was enhanced by the use of legal-adversarial proceedings, which by their nature involve seeking out the 'true facts' from competing expert and lay opinions (Wynne 1982; Hamlin 1986; Massey 1988). Within such procedures, the way lay open to pointing to the official bodies as possessing the facts and the relevant expertise in a way that inquiry objectors could not match.

On the question of what standards should be applied to radioactive discharges to help ensure their 'acceptability', Parker dismissed criticism of the NRPB and ICRP and confirmed that they alone were the proper bodies to assess such matters (Breach 1978 134–5). On radiation risks to Windscale workers in particular, which one objector's expert witness estimated at up to twenty times the currently accepted ICRP and NRPB standards, Parker affirmed that these official bodies could be relied upon to deal with unresolved questions on their own:

> It is probably the case that within two or three years the particular matters advanced by Dr. Stewart will have been resolved and that her conclusions will have been accepted, or proved to be, in part or in whole, ill-founded. (Parker 1978 43)

Parker confirmed BNFL's capacity to satisfy official emission standards despite considerable evidence that it had not always done so in the past (Parker 1978 46). More generally, he emphasized BNFL's twenty-five years of experience in nuclear fuel reprocessing (1978 8); affirmed that the NRPB and the ICRP were 'neutral' and 'independent' bodies whose dual roles of both setting and policing radiation standards need not be separated (1978 58); and argued that a pro-industry bias in such bodies actually might be beneficial in that it would encourage greater stringency on safety matters (1978 62). He felt that some objecting evidence had been 'irrational', 'fanciful' or 'immoderate', at times (when criticizing the authorities) reaching 'a level of absurdity' (1978 33–4 and 62). Far from having to justify in detail their safety criteria, the authorities had their competence to deal independently with such matters confirmed. This is not necessarily to suggest that Parker was unfairly biased, but rather that his report is a distinct example of the 'confirmation' strategy of legitimation.

If the Parker approach was unambiguously confirmatory, Sir Frank Layfield, QC, the Sizewell 'B' PWR inquiry inspector, combined the confirmatory and justificatory paths in a complex manner. He felt that confirmation of the competence of the relevant promotional and regulatory authorities would not be enough on its own. He wrote in his report:

> As a large number of safety aspects had to be left to the NII and the CEGB to resolve as part of the nuclear site licensing process, it was important that my Assessors and I should be satisfied with the reliability and competence of both organizations. Summary volume, (Layfield 1987 s.2.12)

Thus it was for Layfield to examine and if possible establish the competence of the NII, such that 'if the NII decides to grant a nuclear site licence, the Secretary of State must be confident that he can rely on the NII's assessment of those safety issues not examined fully at the inquiry' (1987 Vol. 2, s.4.6). To a far greater extent than at Windscale, the regulatory bodies had to justify themselves in order to be seen to be worthy of public trust. At the end of the day, they were 'confirmed':

> Both organizations (CEGB and NII) showed an impressive degree of technical competence. No significant shortcomings were revealed ... (Summary volume, s. 2.125)

Layfield also concluded that

> there was no evidence or suggestion that the Government's powers of direction had in any way reduced the NII's independence in reaching and carrying its expert judgments on safety matters into effect. (Vol. 2, s. 7.24)

However, confirmation came at a price. The inquiry's scrutiny of the NII and the CEGB on safety went far beyond previous occasions and, apparently, what either body had anticipated. Scrutiny of the premises and methods underpinning the PWR safety case came to focus on the two standard nuclear safety principles. These were ALRA (the risks should be 'as low as reasonably achievable') and ALARP ('as low as reasonably practicable'). Also under review was Probabilistic Risk Assessment (PRA), a computer technique aimed at assessing the probability of a major reactor accident occurring. It is worth remembering that the Three Mile Island accident, involving a PWR, played a special role in focusing attention at the inquiry on safety in general and the utility of these computer models in particular. The Chernobyl disaster – although not involving a PWR – added to this emphasis after the inquiry (but before the publication of the inquiry report).

The study by O'Riordan, Kemp and Purdue (1988) is an exhaustive account of the events, arguments and context of the Sizewell inquiry. In their section on 'safety and public trust', the authors point out that the agenda on risk and safety had moved well beyond the days when scientific 'fact' and value judgments were seen as separable. The 'especially difficult objective' of the inquiry was to:

> devise institutions designed to incorporate the political, the moral, the ideological and the critical discussions of the contemporary risk debate with the technical and the scientific [discussions]. (O'Riordan et al. 1988 184)

Much debate centred on what might constitute an 'acceptable risk' from dangerous releases of radioactivity or major accidents in the reactor core. O'-Riordan et al. set out four criteria which were at times called upon in the effort to pin down the meaning of 'acceptable'. The most important of these are the 'comparison' and 'economic justification' methods. 'Comparison' suggests that risks which 'appear less threatening than other more familiar hazards' are widely accepted (or, more accurately, 'tolerated' for want of a better way of achieving certain benefits). Frequent comparisons in the nuclear debate include risks apparently accepted by motorists and by workers in the coal industry. The argument from economic justification holds that social benefits arising from risky activity can justify acceptance of any residual risks associated with that activity which may remain after all reasonable efforts to reduce risk have been made (O'Riordan et al. 1988 192).

The Sizewell inquiry found that the NII and the CEGB had not put enough thought into the notion of 'acceptability'. Clearly, the acceptability or tolerability of risks additional to those from existing plants and other sources require justification in economic or national interest terms. Initially, the CEGB had not formally taken this into account (O'Riordan *et al.* 1988 196). The inquiry increasingly focused on the ALARP ('as low as reasonably practicable') safety principle as one which the NII in particular should clarify and apply in the future. The authors comment that:

> The important feature of the 'new look' ALARP is its dependence on the justification criterion so central to the concept of acceptable risk. The inquiry only touched on this important issue ... (O'Riordan *et al.* 1988 201)

There is the rub for the NII now. While Layfield affirmed the NII's worthiness and its independence of the industry it regulates, he pressed it to develop the ALARP principle and to publicize the view of the acceptability and tolerability of risk which informs its work. At the core of the ALARP principle is the requirement to weigh risks against benefits. No assessment of risk acceptability using ALARP can be satisfactory without considering benefits flowing from the acceptance of risk. The NII, therefore, is now pressed to move into a political and economic minefield: what are the benefits of nuclear power against other forms of electricity generation? At the same time it must seek to maintain its independence of the industry by leaving the wider discussion of such benefits to others. We return to this dilemma below.

This is just one issue where the Sizewell inquiry took the 'justificatory' and not the 'confirmatory' path toward legitimation of the nuclear safety case. On probabilistic risk assessment (PRA) a complex computer-based method of analysing design reliability, both the NII and the CEGB sought to distance themselves from it in their approach to this subject (O'Riordan *et al.* 1988 214). This was after Friends of the Earth had convincingly argued that PRA is necessarily speculative 'because there is not sufficient reactor experience to apply retrospective appraisal' and that 'conservative' applications of the principle could therefore easily still be over-optimistic about the unlikelihood of an accident occurring (*ibid.*). This was one subject on which the NII was discomforted by the fact that judgments arising from incomplete information necessarily play a role in risk assessment. The nuclear safety agenda in Britain and elsewhere had broadened to include recognition of this fact, adding to the legitimation burden on the Nuclear Inspectorate's shoulders as it emerged from Sizewell.

Finally, Layfield was unhappy with the apparent lack of communication between the NII, the NRPB and CEGB on such matters as how to assess risk. He felt that too little attention had been paid to risk assessment by all concerned, singling out the NII for not taking an interest in the NRPB's efforts to formalize risk – cost – benefit analysis and for relying on generally unspecified, informal rules of thumb. The lack of formal safety criteria irked Layfield and he pressed the NII to formulate and publish its criteria in a publicly digestible form. As noted, he also felt that the Nuclear Inspectorate should address the issue of justification, whether economic or otherwise, in setting out its criteria (O'Riordan *et al.* 1988 203).

The Sizewell inquiry was therefore crucial in a number of respects. Firstly, it was responding to an agenda within which the safety case required much stronger legitimation than before. Secondly, Layfield's critical approach pushed the agenda further in this direction by, for example, making it clear that fully 'scientific' judgments of danger and risk levels were not possible. The post-Sizewell agenda has set considerable new demands in the effort to legitimize the safety case. Thirdly, the CEGB in particular felt that the Sizewell inquiry should have examined the PWR safety case and its economic justification once and for all. The Board and the NII should now be left to look after such matters on their own in the future. This view (had it prevailed) would have ended the public inquiry as the centre-piece of legitimation. (A formal local authority objection to a new generating station makes a public inquiry compulsory under the Electricity Acts: beyond this, the Secretary of State for Energy may opt to submit an application from the generating bodies to an inquiry.) The post-Sizewell, upgraded NII would conceivably carry the burden of legitimation of the PWR safety case into the future. In other words, a further broadening of the agenda had given rise to the need for a 'new', more 'independent' source of advice on safety, namely the upgraded NII. Following on from this, the post-Sizewell era promised to be one of justificatory rather than confirmatory legitimation, the inquiry itself and the Layfield report representing this transition.

The NII's new high profile and heavier burden contrast sharply with its humble beginnings. We must turn now to its changing role in nuclear regulation, including many recent changes in its status and operations. This will lead us to consider whether, in the light of the Hinkley Point inquiry during 1988–9, the legitimating role of the 'big public inquiry' has in fact taken a back seat.

THE NUCLEAR INSTALLATIONS INSPECTORATE

Charting the story of the NII provides an illuminating case study of the shifts that have taken place in the effort to legitimize the nuclear safety case in Britain. The Inspectorate was formed in April 1960 under the provisions of the Nuclear Installations (Licensing and Insurance) Act of 1959. Initially under the Ministry of Power, the NII became part of the Health and Safety Executive in 1974. The terms of its operation are now those set out in the Nuclear Installations Act of 1965, though the formal licensing authority since 1974 is the HSE (Rhodes 1981 262). The law stipulates that those wishing to build or run a commercial (non-research, non-military) nuclear facility must obtain a licence from the HSE. Any licence granted may have conditions attached, 'designed to secure safety both for workers and the general public in the design, siting, construction, installation, operation and maintenance of nuclear plants' (Rhodes 1981 262).

As set out in a HSE document of 1977, the functions of the NII are threefold: to assess the safety aspects of 'new nuclear systems that may be introduced into Great Britain'; to perform safety assessments for specific reactor designs for which the CEGB, the South of Scotland Electricity Board or BNFL (and now also the AEA, as we shall see below) seek a licence; and to inspect installations to 'ensure that the conditions of the licence and any associated subsidiary requirements are met' (HSE

1977). Responsibility for safety remains with the operator or licensee: the Nuclear Installations Act places 'an absolute liability on the licensee to secure that no injury to persons or damage to property is caused by radiation arising from his site' (HSE 1987).

The conventional wisdom is that the creation of the NII was a response to the Windscale fire of 1957 (see for example Fernie and Openshaw 1987 102). This is only partly true, at most. As the title of the Nuclear Installations (Licensing and Insurance) Act of 1959 suggests, its passage was part of a policy for the development of a commercial reactor programmeme in the United Kingdom. It did not affect the status or operations of the research and development programmes: the AEA remained exempt from the need to obtain an NII licence, thought the Inspectorate could inspect AEA sites. Certainly, the Windscale fire speeded the NII's creation, but it did not entail overt criticism, at least, of the AEA's safety record or standards stemming from that accident. In fact, quite the opposite was implied. The Paymaster-General, Reginald Maudling, in moving the second reading of the 1959 Bill, commented:

> In establishing his Inspectorate [the Minister for Power] will, naturally, work in close consultation with the Atomic Energy Authority, which possesses the greatest pool of expert knowledge on this subject ... [The AEA] know most about this thing. One could not possibly have a safety organisation which would tell them what to do about their experimental reactors without knowing as much as they do about the experiments ... as they are dealing with experimental reactors and not the normal commercial type of reactor ... it seems rather pointless to subject them to this statutory licensing system. (*Hansard*, vol. 599, 1959 864).

Like the American Price – Anderson Act of 1957, the 1959 Act sought to make commercial operation more attractive by limiting the absolute liability on operators in the event of an accident. In Britain the limit was set at £5 million.

The marginal status of the NII extended to its staffing: '... nearly all its staff came from the AEA and the nuclear industry; there was no other source of expertise' (Fernie and Openshaw 1987 102). Given the exemption of AEA sites from licensing (though not from inspection) under the Act, this was no direct conflict of interest, though the placing of the NII within the Ministry of Power, which was responsible for the continuing expansion and development of nuclear power among other power sources, clearly was. However, dependence on other arms of the industry for expert staff has been a running problem for the Inspectorate, and its sometime need to second staff from the CEGB (its main regulatee) has long been a source of unease (Fernie and Openshaw 1987 118; *Atom*, April 1989, 22). Resource limitations have perennially stopped the NII carrying out its functions thoroughly and independently in other ways. Until late 1988, for example, it was strongly dependent on the AEA for safety research.

The Inspectorate's low profile persisted until the late 1970s. It did not publish an annual report until 1978; did not publish its safety criteria; and brought no prosecutions under the statutory provisions. Like the machinery of regulation in Britain more generally, the NII's style, and its relationship with its regulatees, was

secretive, consensual and discretionary (O'Riordan *et al.* 1988 187). One pre-
Sizewell exception to its normal style was its report of 1981 *The Management of
Safety at Windscale,* which bluntly criticized BNFL for poor safety standards
(Patterson 1985 131–4). At the Sizewell inquiry, however, the NII was under fire
for having too cosy a relationship with its regulatees:

> Neither the NII nor the HSE has ever fully exposed its philosophy and principles
> before. Indeed, within the inquiry there was much interest and not a little
> amusement to see senior officials actually having to justify, and being closely
> examined upon, principles and assumptions whose origin and purpose had
> never been made clear. (O'Riordan *et al.* 1988 187–8).

Partly in line with the rise of its main regulatee, the CEGB, and the decline of the
AEA, the NII has carried a greater share of the burden of legitimizing the safety case
in recent years. As we have noted, the Sizewell inquiry saw the use of both the
'confirmatory' and 'justificatory' legitimation techniques, reflecting the broadening of the nuclear agenda. The NII's role in the era of AEA dominance and
'legitimation by default' was marginal; it was hardly less so at the height of the
confirmatory approach at the Windscale inquiry. But the further broadening of the
agenda in the 'Sizewell era' demanded continual 'justificatory' legitimation of the
nuclear safety case, above and beyond periodical public inquiries. How the NII
would cope with its higher profile and greater burden was an open question. The
chief NII official, Edward Ryder, was cited in the House of Commons debate on the
Layfield report as saying that, given understaffing, the NII's choice was to 'reduce
standards or delay work'.

The NII's heightened role is evident in a number of recent events. It has
conducted Long Term Safety Reviews of the CEGB's ageing Magnox reactors as a
part of the process of phasing them out (the Berkeley station was shut down in April
1989) and it has stated an intention to make these reviews a condition for all licensed
nuclear power reactors (HSE 1987). After almost thirty-five years of exemption
from the licensing process, the AEA in September 1988 was required retrospectively
to obtain site licences from the HSE / NII, ostensibly because the Authority was now
operating as a trading fund and should be treated the same as others operating
commercially (*Atom,* November 1988, 2; *The Independent,* 15 September 1988).
However, this was one in a series of blows to the once-formidable AEA, the greatest
of which was the virtual cessation of government funding of the Fast Breeder
Reactor programmeme, announced in July 1988 (*The Independent,* 22 July 1988).
Further, in October 1988, the Secretary of State for Energy announced that in future
the HSE would decide what nuclear safety research should be carried out and would
be given the power to impose a charge on the operators to cover its costs. After
April 1990, when these changes would be complete, the HSE's total research budget
would be double its previous level. In the nuclear safety field, the research gains
of the HSE were mostly at the expense of the AEA's Safety and Reliability Directorate (*The Independent,* 28 October 1988; *Atom,* January 1989). This virtually ends
the AEA's role in PWR safety research.

On top of all this, the NII began to flex its muscles in an unprecedented manner.
It threatened to shut down parts of BNFL's reprocessing facilities at Sellafield if a

number of changes were not made to reduce radiation doses to plant workers. John Rimington, the Director-General of the HSE, has commented that, whereas in 1981 the Executive had issued recommendations to BNFL, in 1986 it was issuing instructions (*Guardian,* 12 December 1986). Then, in February 1989, the NII instigated charges against the South of Scotland Board for lacking sufficient emergency back-up diesel generation (*Guardian,* 3 February 1989). Amid continuing worries over the HSE / NII's capacity to carry out its old and new functions, the Government planned extra resources for the NII, notably the recruitment of twenty further professional inspectors (*The Independent,* 15 September 1988). This move was accompanied by a 17 per cent pay increase for inspectors to make the NII more competitive in the job market: well above the government's pay norms for the public sector generally. The NII was thus being equipped to be the authoritative source of advice on nuclear safety at a time of considerable change (the replacement of Magnox capacity by the PWR and the impending proposed privatization of nuclear electricity supply, although the latter did not, in fact, occur).

In response to Layfield's demand for explicit safety criteria, the HSE published a 36-page document, *The Tolerability of Risk from Nuclear Power Stations,* in 1988. It represents a valiant attempt to meet the legitimation burden posed by the broadened agenda, and shows the HSE / NII grappling with the new consensus that science cannot answer all the important questions about nuclear safety and risk. It also shows the NII trying to duck issues at the core of the ALARP principle; understandably so, perhaps, since it needs above all to be seen as an independent and objective source of safety advice to the industry. Events before and during the Hinkley Point inquiry of 1988–9 show that the 'limits of science' and 'nature of ALARP' problems continue to trouble the Inspectorate.

The NII's *Tolerability* (not, we may note, 'acceptability') document claims to be a 'straightforward account written for the general public' (HSE 1988 1). It starts from the premise that the likes of nuclear risks are not areas of judgment 'for experts alone'. Most important, it seeks to explain the ALARP principle, whereby if a risk falls between being unacceptably large and so small as to be of no real concern, it should be reduced 'to a level which is as low as reasonably practicable' (p. 4). No full critique of the document will be attempted here, but we will concentrate on the question of balancing risks and benefits within ALARP.

The area where ALARP is applicable to risk assessment involves society tolerating a residual risk arising from an activity, where that residual risk adds to the risks citizens already run from a range of other sources and activities. The risk can be tolerable if it can be justified in terms of the benefits it brings, or will bring, to society. The *Tolerability* document is quite clear on this:

> Whenever we do something that involves taking a risk – even stepping off a pavement when there is traffic – we usually do so because we believe there is some *benefit* that outweighs it ... [This paper] concentrates on certain kinds of risk that are regulated by society as a whole, with the aim of securing general benefits ... [ALARP means] bearing in mind the benefits flowing from acceptance [of risk] and taking into account the costs of further reduction ... (HSE 1988 1,4)

It continues later:

> A judgment also depends upon consideration of the alternatives. In judging the
> nuclear risk, we have to bear in mind that the hazards, in terms of ecological
> and climatic impact and health dangers, of extracting and burning fossil fuels
> to produce an equivalent amount of electricity, are considerable. (HSE 1988 26)

There are three key elements to ALARP: risk, the cost of reducing risk, and the
benefits flowing from accepting risk. Layfield wanted the NII to make more use of
cost – benefit analysis (CBA) (O'Riordan *et al.* 1988 218), but the Inspectorate is
wary of this technique, given long-recognized difficulties of assigning comparable
money values to disparate phenomena (such as time saved, comfort, convenience,
environmental disruption, etc.) (HSE 1988, Appendix B). This is one obstacle to
seeing benefits as exhausted in the set of benefits flowing from reduced risk. The
reduction of risk is certainly a benefit, but it does not justify the imposition on
society of the residual risk. ALARP requires a broader view of benefits flowing from
the acceptance or toleration of risk. This would necessarily include consideration
of the putative social, economic and political benefits of nuclear power, both on its
own terms and compared to alternative forms of generation. The *Tolerability*
document hesitates at this point. As noted, it comments on the need to compare
nuclear and fossil fuel risks (why not renewable sources as well?). But it concludes:
'It is not however for the regulatory authorities but for the public to weigh the
benefits of nuclear power with the risks we have outlined' (HSE 1988 26). This
reluctance to address benefits in the fuller sense has led to the HSE / NII being
pressed openly to discuss the benefits of nuclear power. The HSE / NII's governing
body, the Health and Safety Commission, has supported their reluctance to step
into this minefield. The Commission's chairman has commented:

> We agree with the Executive that the consideration of the benefits of nuclear
> power as a whole is not appropriate for the regulatory body. It should be
> concerned with setting the conditions for safety. (quoted in *Atom,* October
> 1988, 29)

This runs against the views of Layfield and the nuclear industry (*Atom,* October
1988, 29; see also O'Riordan *et al.* 1988 203 and Layfield 1987 Summary volume
s. 2.71) reinforcing the contradictory nature of the demands for independence and
benefit-assessment being laid on the NII. Those within the industry have no qualms
about arguing for the benefits of nuclear power in the risk assessment equation (see
for example Saunders in *Atom,* December 1988, 7–10).

This dilemma is a strong impediment to the NII taking its place as the 'new'
source of advice on safety within the new, tougher safety agenda. It is also the main
factor impeding the completion of the shift from 'confirmatory' to 'justificatory'
legitimation of the safety case. In addition to these problems, the NII came under
considerable pressure at the Hinkley Point 'C' inquiry conducted by Michael
Barnes, QC. The NII has had its belief that the public is prepared to tolerate the
chance of a significant nuclear accident once every 10,000 years challenged by the
NRPB director who confirmed his organization's view that one accident every
100,000 years is 'the limit of individual tolerated risk' (*Guardian,* 13 February
1989). The HSE's Director-General conceded at the inquiry that no responses from

members of the general public to the *Tolerability* document had been received (*Planning,* 10 February 1989). Worse still, a former HSE mining engineer inspector strongly criticized the Executive's approach to risk assessment, including its failure to 'clarify how the economic benefits of nuclear power could be judged against risk' (*Guardian,* 27 March 1989). Barnes and his expert assessors had expressed 'scepticism' about the Executive's (and the CEGB's) risk estimates (*Guardian,* 27 March 1989).

On present evidence, the Hinkley Point 'C' inquiry represents in itself a heightening of demands on the nuclear regulatory agencies. The questionable economic justification of nuclear power against alternatives will postpone (and may end) the planned expansion of the British nuclear programmeme: a Government review is currently planned for 1994. It may even come to spell the phasing out of the nuclear programmeme as a whole. If there are to be further nuclear power stations in Britain, the NII must carry the bulk of the safety legitimation burden. Future plants would be built for the new state-owned company Nuclear Electric PLC. Sam Goddard, Head of Construction and Future Programmemes at Nuclear Electric and CEGB's former nuclear chief planner, had expressed the hope that 'a public inquiry would not be necessary for a second Sizewell PWR (Sizewell C) because plans for the first PWR had already been subjected to thorough examination' (The *Financial Times,* 1 February 1989). Both Sizewell C and Wylfa PWR now await the 1994 review. But if they or any other stations are ever actually proposed by Nuclear Electric, then the demands on the NII will be very high. Legitimation of the safety case will have to flow for the most part from the Inspectorate's demonstrated competence and the adequacy of its criteria, since the major confirming role of public inquiries, at least on the question of design safety, would be reduced or removed. One thing is certain. The burden of the nuclear safety case on the NII is several times greater than that on its, and the AEA's, shoulders up to twenty years before.

SUMMARY AND CONCLUSIONS

This chapter has argued that, in order to legitimize the nuclear safety case in Britain, the source and style of advice to government on safety changed in line with the broadening of the nuclear power agenda. As the burden of legitimation grew, the source and style of safety advice altered accordingly.

In terms of its source, the shift was in essence from the AEA to the big inquiry and, perhaps, thence to the NII. In terms of style, it shifted from secrecy and legitimation 'by default' to the 'confirmation' of the source, thence to the 'justification' of the competence of the source. Nuclear Electric and its allies face an uphill battle to convince the government that any new stations should be built. This continuing uncertainty means that the shifting in source and style of advice are not complete. This state of flux in part reflects the sheer weight of the burden inherited by the NII and the vagaries of, among other things, risk assessment.

Successive British governments have been pushed, by necessity, to accept an increasingly demanding legitimation burden on nuclear power. In the end, the strength and longevity of governmental commitment to nuclear power will be the key factor in determining whether the tougher agenda of today can be adequately dealt with by the NII, by public inquiries, or both.

Atom, Journal of the United Kingdom Atomic Energy Authority.

Blowers, A. and Pepper, D. (1987), The nuclear state: from consensus to conflict; in Blowers and Pepper (eds), *Nuclear Power in Crisis* (London: Croom Helm).

Breach, I. (1978), *Windscale Fallout* (Harmondsworth: Penguin).

Fernie, J. and Openshaw, S. (1987), A comparative analysis of nuclear plant regulation in the US and UK; in Blowers and Pepper (eds), *op. cit.*

Fleck (Sir) A. (1958), Reports, Cmnd 338 and 471 (Chairman: Sir A. Fleck).

Gowing, M. (1974), *Independence and Deterrence* (London: Macmillan).

Hall, T. (1986), *Nuclear Politics* (Harmondsworth: Penguin).

Hamlin, C. (1986), Scientific method and expert witnessing: Victorian perspectives on a modern problem; *Social Studies of Science,* 16, 485–513.

Hansard (1959), vol. 599.

Health and Safety Executive (1977), *Some Aspects of the Safety of Nuclear Installations in Great Britain* (London: HMSO).

Health and Safety Executive (1987), *Bradwell Nuclear Power Station* (London: HMSO).

Health and Safety Executive (1988), *The Tolerability of Risk from Nuclear Power Stations* (London: HMSO).

Layfield, (Sir) F. (1987), *Sizewell B Public Inquiry: Report* (6 vols plus Summary volume) (London: HMSO).

Lowe, P. and Goyder, J. (1983), *Environmental Groups in Politics* (Hemel Hempstead: Allen & Unwin).

Massey, A. (1986), Professional elites and BNFL; *Politics,* 6,1.

Massey, A. (1988), *Technocrats and Nuclear Politics: the influence of professional experts in policy-making* (Farnborough: Avebury).

O'Riordan, T. Kemp, R. and Purdue, M. (1988), *Sizewell B: An anatomy of the inquiry* (London: Macmillan).

Parker, (Sir) R. (1978), *The Windscale Inquiry: Report* (London: HMSO).

Patterson, W. (1985), *Going Critical* (London: Grafton Books).

Planning (1989), (Gloucester: Ambit Publications).

Rhodes, G. (1981), *Inspectors in British Government* (London: Allen & Unwin).

UK Atomic Energy Authority (1984), *The Development of Atomic Energy 1939–1984: Chronology of events* (UKAEA).

Valentine, J. (1985), *Atomic Crossroads* (London: Merlin).

Williams, R. (1980), *The Nuclear Power Decisions* (London: Croom Helm).

Wynne, B. (1982), *Rationality and Ritual* (Chalfont St Giles: The British Society for the History of Science).

Seven

The State as a Blind Investor in Fundamental Research
Advice to the French and Other Governments on the European Synchrotron Radiation Facility

JEAN TOURNON

This study of a major scientific spending decision has double interest for the theme of expert advice to governments on scientific issues. The problems for State decision-makers in dealing with 'Big Science' funding and its attendant advisory process are severe to the the point of pathology, as this chapter's account of the synchrotron saga illustrates so well. When the project is for fundamental and pure research its very purpose is almost impenetrable to all except handfuls of expert enthusiasts (and, sometimes, expert detractors) who offer rival advice, usually heavily laced with professional self-interest. By contrast, the potential practical value of some commercial invention such as the fast breeder nuclear reactor or a major new weapons system such as the anti-ballistic missile, can be roughly appreciated by the lay decision-maker. With pure research projects, devising criteria for judging whether the proposed design will 'work' – hard enough for nuclear reactors or rocketry – is almost as opaque because the 'results' of the proposed fundamental research will have no practical status which anyone can foresee, however optimistically or imaginatively they may try. So national pride and deference to scientific discovery, particularly in physics, must carry the day with the ministry of finance as well as the ministry of science of the country in question. Jean Tournon's example of the synchrotron project is typical of any advanced country which could contemplate such a scheme. The problems, official reactions, advice processes and decision methods are similar and about equally intractable.

The West European level of this case, however – based on the European Science Foundation and the other governments – doubles the value of the study because it shows how ambitious promoters and advisers can seek to manipulate both the national and international levels of decision-making to get a policy for a project approved and

funded by either or both of them. Jean Tournon's interpretation is that
the West European scientists' pro-synchrotron lobby took their case up
to the ESF as a pincer movement to press their own governments into a
collaborative and possibly cost-sharing agreement with other governments. After several years of 'hide and seek' by these governments,
Federal Germany and France decided to proceed together, with France
settling the siting question. Those with knowledge of federal systems
are familiar with the idea of lobbyists playing to the federal authority in
the hope of stimulating the states or Länder to take action or approve
some funding: it is not so easy in unitary systems with a single government authority.

   In the end, the siting issue was settled within France by the rather
older arts of political patronage, although the story still continues: the
synchrotron is nearly ten years behind its original schedule and still
being built. This study of very costly, yet speculative, expenditure
committed on the basis of unavoidably weak and subjective 'advice' (or
lobbyists' persuasion) may be considered a pathological case of 'expert
advice on scientific policy issues'. But this term may imply that a cure
can be found and applied when it probably cannot. Jean Tournon's image
of the policy-making process as the 'blind investor' – permanently
disabled, rather than only temporarily diseased – is therefore better.

POLICY ADVISING ON FUNDAMENTAL RESEARCH

Nowhere in the world is fundamental scientific research self-supporting or significantly reliant on private financing. Its dependence on public funds makes it an
archetype of politically decided matters, since only a small fraction of all possible
fundamental research eventually gets finance. This problem area is not prominent
in the general public debates in Western democracies and its share in the press or
parliamentary discussions is a good deal smaller, one may guess, than its share of
the public budget. This may be explained by fundamental scientific research being
at once esoteric, very technical and very fragmented in its many and varied forms.
It is also sacred (only barbarians could speak up against research) and 'corporatist'
in the sense that the government decision-makers have a traditional preference for
approving a certain amount for all such research and then letting the scientists
distribute it among themselves. All the same, governments have to make decisions,
big and small, formal or substantive, on fundamental research; this chapter will
consider the peculiar character of the information governments may receive on
such matters.

   Governments have come to understand that they must pay for fundamental
research and also that they have to work very hard if they are to avoid making these
payments as a mere 'blind' investment – that is, an investment based on too little
information and so difficult in its nature as almost to defy rational analysis. In the
short term, governments are pressed by an impressive array of research institutions
and individual research celebrities wanting a budget increase, each one cogently
demonstrating that his activity is presently under-financed and thus under-produc-
tive. Such a clamour aims at ensuring that the present budget will, at least, be
maintained next year; at laying the groundwork for negotiating some increment

here and there; and, last but not least, at keeping alive a hope of triumphal expansion at some future time. Indeed, in the long term, were it not for the resigned attitude or lack of drive of some scientists, the accumulated financial dreams of the research institutions and would-be institutions could easily exceed the total resources of the State. The expedient of trying once again simply to repeat this year's budget next year, even though it does avoid a lot of conflict, is not an admirable way of running things, especially in the ever-changing field of research policy. As a first step, a decision to increase or decrease the total funds for scientific research can be made by the politicians. As usual, they will combine some pragmatism (given the general fiscal scene, the public mood and any current media craze affecting 'science') with some ideology. But they then find themselves at a loss to decide on the kinds, the levels and the aims of this research work to be done, by whom and at what price. This is because, more than other policy fields, this one is, at the same time, fragmented, opaque and unpredictable.

The fragmentation between and within the scientific disciplines is notorious. It is expressed as fields and sub-fields, research organizations, the 'schools of thought' and even the clans or fiefs of leading figures. It follows that the corporatist or peer group way of research funding and management is not really suitable because all scientists do not form one corporation. From one walk of research to another they have nothing in common except their allegiance to 'science' and their scrambling for money from the same public coffer. Scientific research is opaque, at least to those outside the particular sub-field or specialism in question. This is partly because, for reasons of competition, nobody exactly or promptly reports on their current work and thinking. But even so, the focusing of research activity on the 'advancing' of science makes communications between the researcher and the observer very important, although also quite uneasy. This is particularly so when the observer is supposed to guide, evaluate and fund the researcher. The politicians or administrators are not, of course, themselves responsible for the opacity of a policy sector which they pretend to oversee while not being conversant with it. This opacity is almost as great for the scientists themselves because the fundamental research activities of the demographer, the linguist, the botanist, *et al.* are all mutually very difficult to grasp and even impenetrable. (The fundamental research of some political scientists is opaque even to their closest colleagues.) As to unpredictability, any conjecture about fundamental research in, say, twenty years' time is hopeless and the idea of politically engineering some deliberate course in this general trend does not seem realistic for even the wealthiest governments. But for a government simply to facilitate foreseeable trends is not without its risks of side-effects. Short-term investments on particular research projects are filled with uncertainty by the very nature of all fundamental research: the product may be unexpected results (or none at all) and even expected and useful results can find themselves overtaken or put into the shade by the results of other projects, perhaps in other countries.

Ministers are expected to decide their scientific research budget on the basis of some 'research policy' and would, indeed, feel uncomfortable without one. But making such a policy is a *tour de force* because the usual methods of gathering and processing information, of setting goals and of reviewing performance are hardly applicable. For example, a review of past practice is of little use because it is no sure indicator of future needs or likely performance. Consequently, it seems (at least in the case of France) that the Ministry in charge of scientific research exerts, in the routine course of things, little of its policy-making power. The structure of this field of activity permits only indirect and slow influence. Within the big institutions of scientific research, any power to nominate the directors or governing boards which the Government may have is counteracted by the power of internal, national and international systems of peer group judgment and hierarchy. Even the Government's financial sway – the power of the purse – is felt only if the institution is in overall financial straits and suffering such internal rigidities that it cannot transfer funds or cross-subsidize its projects without the Government's detailed knowledge in order to protect its autonomy. As for smaller research institutions, their number and sensitivity make them difficult targets for policy at the ministerial level. However, more influence is wielded by the Ministry when it can oversee and finance the launching of particular new projects which are either too new or too big to be sheltered within the budgets of existing research institutions or when they have been contractually set up and are thus more explicitly shaped and influenced by the Government's policy-makers. It is on the basis of such a case – when governments have more say on the ways and means of fundamental research because a big new project is coming up – that we will examine how information and advice is conveyed, upon demand or not, to the government. The particular fundamental research project for discussion is the synchrotron radiation laboratory of such size and novelty that it was thought, from the beginning, that only the joint efforts of several European governments could bring it into existence.

SYNCHROTRON RADIATION WITHIN THE WESTERN EUROPEAN POLICY ADVICE STRUCTURES

Synchrotron radiation illustrates perfectly the frailty of governments trying to plan fundamental scientific research. The radiation in question is electronic-magnetic, like radio or light waves, rather than associated with nuclear radioactivity. It occurs naturally among the denser stars but also appeared as an unexpected side-effect of using particle accelerators at very high energy for the fundamental study of matter. For the scientists building and operating accelerators, this radiation was also an unwelcome discovery because it represented a loss of energy. A first reasonable action would have been to wage war upon it. Governments could have been advised to pour more money into the design of better adjusted machines to rid them of this unwanted side-effect. No scientists advised going in the other direction of en-couraging and exploiting this bizarre radiation effect. Fortunately, high energy physicists did not complain about this synchrotron radiation and government funding agencies and policy-makers ignored it, perhaps because they could afford to leave room for serendipity. They allowed some marginal research into this phenomenon and during the 1970s it was revealed as an exceptional tool in a wide variety of different fields. The eruption of synchrotron radiation within fundamental photon research produced a number of cleavages between the different vested interests among different types of scientists. Firstly, among the high energy physicists themselves, the few who had founded this new branch of experimental work were opposed by the orthodox majority who (after having conceded a tiny share of their resources to it) discovered that they had nurtured a competitor for big money and big machines. A growing number of scientists, running beyond physics into biology, chemistry, geology and in the applied sciences for calibration and imaging, divided themselves between those who bet for and those who bet against the chances of synchrotron radiation proving a major new technique opening important new applications.

At this point some public policy on the synchrotron was unavoidable because here was an additional instrument for the fundamental investigation of matter. Its emergence confirmed once again the seemingly natural expansionist tendency of fundamental scientific research and the consequential need for governments to curb it, not because of obscurantism but rather the simple finite limits of any public science budget. In shaping some new public policy on this new subject, information could be provided only by the very scientists who were involved in the existing efforts to expand or contain synchrotron radiation research. Only they were competent to discuss the costs and benefits of this new line of research but they had already taken professional sides and were, in particular, well aware of the zero-sum-gain nature of the continual scientific contests for research grants. If new work on synchrotrons received a lot more money, someone else's work would probably receive much less. Technical advice which is heavy with professional self-interest seems inherent and inevitable in the field of fundamental scientific research policy. This might be an extremely efficient basis for policy-making if the advice came exclusively from a unique and privileged source. But this is far from the reality in France. Instead there is a multiplicity of sources of advice and expertise implying both formal and implicit representations of interest. These include specialized groups in the Centre National de la Récherche Scientifique and the universities and the board of the Commissariat à l'Energie Atomique who will first hear the pros and cons and report them to the Ministry of Research and Technology. A 'mission scientifique et technique', with its specialized departments, will discuss it again and submit recommendations to the Minister. But that is just the beginning of the advice ballet. The Ministry of Research and Technology tries to develop its own expertise, including its experts coming in for limited secondments from the science milieu, use of regular civil servants (who, interestingly enough, have often started their career in the scientific community) and of the Minister's special advisers who are formally members of his departmental cabinet or informally located somewhere in the structures of organized science, but in a position to offer the Minister their knowledge and opinions.

In the earlier stage of the particular issue of building a synchrotron, this established 'in-house' advisory apparatus operated normally, taking in the no-doubt abundant supply of information and argument from the various interests. An *ad hoc* advisory committee of ten scientists was appointed by the Ministry of Research and Technology in November 1981 to inquire and report. None of them was a specialist in the field or directly involved in the various national and international projects or schemes for synchrotron research (Comité scientifique 1982). In addition, during the year before the French decision was made, the Minister of Research and Technology arranged for two officials (both scientists) to be in charge of the synchrotron issue; each was said to favour a different solution. These two advisers worked together, each checking the other's different opinion as they submitted material to the Minister. As a trained physicist himself, the Minister took a personal interest. At the levels of Prime Minister and President, however, there were also two advisers (as on all important current policy questions) but each was ignorant of the other's identity and contribution: they each knew only that they shared this advisory role with someone else. (In fact, at that time, the Prime Minister's office was run in this way in imitation of the President's ; (Grenoble 1986.) While not lacking in the quantity of advice and having tried to gauge non-specialist expert opinion from the advisory committee of ten, the Government still lacked good information from outside a narrow band of specialist knowledge and interest on this subject.

THE EUROPEAN SCIENCE FOUNDATION STRATEGY, 1977–9

In the long and tortuous story of the European Synchrotron Radiation Facility, two periods are reviewed here as they show interesting traits in the creation and use of knowledge for public policy. The first period was when the main initiators of synchrotron radiation in Europe concocted an unusual, even brilliant, strategy of directing advice towards their national governments *via* an international body: the ESF. The second period was when the French Government, having received a *carte blanche* on the synchrotron project, agonized about other governments' and its own positions. At first sight, this ESF strategy may appear odd in that the most senior French scientists whom the synchrotron enthusiasts needed to impress are seated *ex officio* in the councils of the ESF, just as they are in France's own national scientific community. To go through the ESF was not, therefore, a strategy designed to avoid or by pass these leading authorities. Rather, it was a means of reaching them from a different and easy direction because international collaboration on such a major project is both scientifically and financially attractive. The ESF is an international body open to 'any national organization of a European country which supports basic research from money assigned ... mainly by the government' (ESF 1975 18). Of course, in each country's national research funding agencies, senior physicists are well established. In France, indeed, the most senior position in the CNRS belongs, no doubt by divine right, to physicists. But the synchrotron's promoters must have thought that their senior French physicist colleagues would feel better able to show support in a collaborative setting of the ESF. Perhaps also, this setting might draw together the very best synchrotron researchers in Western Europe who would produce detailed designs and a working scheme. This ESF-based prospectus would, therefore, have the best chance of attracting the support of the leading lights of science not only in France itself but from across Western Europe.

Approaching their goal *via* the ESF was a clever strategic move by the synchrotron's promoters *vis-à-vis* their relationships not only with mainstream physicists (within and beyond France) but also their synchrotron research colleagues in other countries. Some of these may have lacked enthusiasm and been satisfied with the gradual unfolding of the new technology and its financial fortunes. They may even have tacitly accepted the disapproving scepticism about synchrotron work from some of their fellow physicists in their own countries or institutions. The collaborative ESF setting attracted those who believed that synchrotron radiation was a quite different and unique process or method, offering almost unlimited investigative capacity, and who therefore wanted the best possible machine. Such a machine could be afforded by no single European country. The partisans of a new research field which could be seen as both somewhat marginal and potentially profligate had every incentive to try to operate on the high ground of European collaboration. ESF was the body whose powerful international advice would carry forward governments, professional opponents and the more timid professional allies towards the desired goal.

The ESF's advice structure on the subject was begun with a working party which reported to the General Assembly of the Foundation in November 1977 (ESF 1977). *Synchrotron radiation – a perspective view for Europe* recommended a feasibility study for a European synchrotron laboratory. The Assembly accepted this idea and immediately established an *ad hoc* committee to prepare this study. Eighteen months later the Assembly and its Executive Council received a four-volume, 600-page report combining technical minutiæ with the enthusiastic sentiments of the scientific pioneer – 'each time a new source of radiation has appeared, new fields of science have opened and important discoveries have been made' (ESF 1979 9). The Foundation's leading scientific advisers and delegates did indeed put their stamp of approval on to the scheme, conveying to their members' respective governments their 'strong recommendation that ways and means should be sought to turn these exciting proposals into a European reality' (ESF 1979 7). This advice was prestigious and highly public but it is worth noting that it was perhaps rather formal, even ceremonial, given the dual status of the leading scientists who had endorsed it as ESF policy and who would then repeat this view as senior advisers to their own governments. The recommendation was, however, also unsolicited. But it came to each government with the familiar names of their own national expert advisers associated with it and carried the ESF's overall *imprimatur.*

As the practical document, culminating in an actual synchrotron outline design, the ESF's feasibility study committee's report was, of course, crucial to the synchrotron's success. It would stand as the sole authoritative outline of the preferred European design. It would attract the allegiance of the whole synchrotron research community (perhaps even of physicists at large who would recognize a good physics-based cause); consign to oblivion the various less ambitious 'favourite son' national synchrotron projects which could threaten that country's participation in a bigger collaborative project; and impress national governments, the scientific peers in other research fields and policy arenas – plus the mass media – so that a favourable climate was created. In fact, the report, in its four volumes, succeeded very well. It has had no competitor as the true guide to the synchrotron's actual form. It 'designed' a much better and costlier machine than it had originally conceived as the committee went along by the amiable process of offering and accepting new ideas for extra features and capacities during its missionary journey, or advertising campaign, among some 120 European scientists within atomic and molecular physics, chemistry, materials science and life sciences who were gathered into eleven specialist workshops to discuss how they would like to use such a machine in their work if one was built (ESF 1979 15). The committee was clearly engaged on a demand-raising and clientele-formation exercise at least as much as an inquiry and design task. If they were planning to build a machine for a constituency, they saw the need first to establish a constituency. This would be entirely on a European base, of course, for it was only on that base that the political will or the money could be found. European pride was important. The Foundation had instructed the committee to devise a synchrotron laboratory which 'should approach the final state of the art' (ESF 1977). The committee could now affirm in its own report that the scheme as proposed, 'by its performance will keep Europe in an outstanding position in the field of synchrotron radiation ... In addition, it will make a strong, positive contribution to the development of both interdisciplinary research and European collaboration' (ESF 1979 62).

FIVE YEARS OF GOVERNMENTAL HIDE-AND-SEEK, 1979–1984

Unfortunately for the synchrotron's promoters, this distinguished advice could not galvanize any European decision-maker into action. In the spring of 1979 there was no European-level science or research and development policy or budget nor any authority competent to decide on such a scheme. When the problem of governments not possessing the information they need for policy-making is so commonly noted, perhaps here is an example of information not possessing the government it needs. Whether advice of this kind from a source such as the ESF was premature or the creation of the European policy for science was tardy, the fact was that the Foundation could do no more than circulate its recommendation for the synchrotron to the national decision-makers in its members' respective countries. These decision-makers belied this description of them during a five-year period of hide-and-seek which produced no outcome. The committee had hoped for construction work to begin by 1980 and operations by 'about 1985'(ESF 1979 7).

The project is now almost ten years later than this proposal: major parts of the architectural design were rejected in mid-1988 and 1989 became the earliest possible starting date, with actual operations loosely projected for perhaps 1993.

The dozen participating governments were in a standard game relationship to each other on the question of who would pay for the synchrotron and who would get it build on their soil. Each player wanted to minimize his payments but see the facility come to his country (to the benefit of its national scientific facilities, its prestige and its inward investment flow). The game was played by much national posturing, notably a due deference to the scheme's pioneering scientific value and the daring vision of its creators, combined with the earnest hope that Europe would, indeed, seize this opportunity to put her scientists ahead in international scientific competition. No clearer proof of this commitment could be offered than each country's readiness to welcome this large investment on to its own territory. Of course, the synchrotron was not the only European scientific issue in play during these years of devious haggling about it, nor even the only major fixed scientific investment which would need to find a home on some acceptable political and financial terms. With almost every aspect of more than one project capable of being made contingent on almost every other – cost and overall design, national shares of cost, construction contracts, siting, future use, etc. – the scope for indecisive hide-and-seek was very great.

FRANCE AND GERMANY ACT TOGETHER

Culminating in an agreement between them in the summer of 1984, the Federal German and French Governments sought to settle the issue by promising to find the major funding for the synchrotron between them. It was one of two major research facilities under European negotiation at that time and was 'devolved', under the agreement of 1984, to France for further progress and execution. A clear indication of the agreement between the two new principal paymasters was that this machine could stand in France on a site chosen by the French. This clarification of the matter in the minds of some ten other governments greatly altered the game but did not end it. France and Germany did not want to pay all the cost so some negotiation with others remained due. As the game's designated organizer, the French Government wanted to know of each other government whether it would participate in the new form of the project if so, on what terms and what share of the cost it would accept. Common sense might suggest that only this question of payment need have been posed: if the offerings from others did not fill the remaining gap in the subscription list, the French and Germans could either have increased their own sums and gone ahead together, or finally given up. But seasoned national government officials will not talk about money until its context is clear so the other terms of their participation were still important. Denmark and Italy, for example, had long been pressing their own sites for the synchrotron and would not give them up too readily in negotiations about money, even though the Franco-German agreement had probably doomed them.

For any and all of the other governments, the bilateral decision of the two most committed and wealthy countries was a sensitive matter. While not secret, it had not been formally notified to (much less offered for consultation among) the other governments who were all still, formally, negotiating with the French and German Governments, as well as among themselves, about this project. So, if the two leading countries still wanted others' subscriptions, they had to tolerate a further period of game-playing about money, all closely tied in with practical matters concerning the machine's nature and use, the legal basis of payments and user agreements and, even now, the question of a site – perhaps, even, other governments' views on a site within France. The other governments had, therefore, both financial and symbolic reasons for pretending that the hide-and-seek was continuing, even though the two major players had already found each other and were trying to end the game in order to build the synchrotron. A certain amount of talk of a 'community' approach was employed to convey some resentment against the Franco-German agreement while guarding national positions on subscriptions. The potential danger for the project and its two leading national patrons was that, even at this stage, there could have been enough friction and difficulty to cause France and Germany to abort the project rather than either pay virtually the full cost or suffer political damage which would have spilled over into other fields and issues of possibly greater importance. This danger even applied to the French Government's choice of a French site, partly because the French themselves did not appear unanimous on the question.

THE GRENOBLE SITING DECISION – SCARCE INFORMATION AND 'BLIND INVESTING' IN FUNDAMENTAL SCIENTIFIC RESEARCH

In essence, there would seem to have been no issue arising outside France on the siting of the machine within France: the agreement with the Federal German Government was clear. But this agreement had been reached in the context of a Strasbourg site which, the Germans would have noted, was nearer to their relevant scientific centres than to the French ones. The French Government was publicly committed to 'defend before its European partners the candidacy of Strasbourg' (Strasbourg 1983; Alsace 1985) but this was not a promise to impose it against any and all opposition. Paris had been discussed, but rejected on strategic land-use planning grounds, and Lille and Lorraine both also mentioned, while the other candidate was Grenoble, enjoying noticeable support from some scientists in the field, including those of Britain and Germany who had enjoyed collaborating at other facilities at Grenoble since 1972. Even though the French Government was not hostile to a Strasbourg site, could it come off from Strasbourg, in Grenoble's favour, without straining the agreement with the Germans and even risking the entire project if various other contingencies combined negatively together?

By the autumn of 1984, soon after the Franco-German Agreement had become known, the French Government was receiving a flurry of formal or informal, solicited or unsolicited and widely discordant opinions and pieces of information about the siting decision. There was nothing unusual in this variegated flow of intelligence: all significant issues generate it (Tournon 1988). But in the academic context of expert advice to governments on scientific issues, it is salutary to note how much general (including even brutally political) 'advice' a government also receives whenever a decision is to be made which will produce costs and benefits and how 'scientific issues' come down to very ordinary physical and administrative decisions, at least when they move towards practical implementation. From the 'partner' governments and countries on the synchrotron project came the information and views of the ministers of science themselves, either speaking privately to the French Minister or, unattributably, to journalists or the other participants in the debate. These others included senior officials and internal advisers in the various ministries of science, nationally eminent scientists in both France and the other interested countries, heads of national or international scientific research organizations (notably, of course, the European Science Foundation) diplomats and interested politicians – all doing the same as the ministers by declaring their official positions on the record and then speaking to each other and to journalists on a private or unattributable basis. All had something to tell, or urge, on the future of the synchrotron.

Within the French Government, the policy community of this kind of scientific research and the wider political system – not least those parts representing Strasbourg and Grenoble – there were even further layers of circuits, relays and targets. The Minister of Research, the Prime Minister and the President, each with their systems of dual advisers, formed the other strata with lines of co-operation and cleavage below them involving their own respective officials (lay administrators, scientists, finance controllers); synchrotron specialists still opposed by other physicists; physicists contrasted with other types of scientist; the CNRS and other research bodies – not to mention the other world of local politicians and city officials pressing the cases for Strasbourg and Grenoble. Knowing that the French siting decision was still to be fought for, the professional and local interests did their best to transmit, amplify and, if necessary, create information on every aspect of the issue. The suggestion that the partner governments would insist upon or refuse some point was an easy line to shoot as so little was definite on the international front. The French Government still lacked clear information, despite this *claque* , because only the German position was fairly clear – and a move from Strasbourg might be claimed as grounds for throwing even that into new doubt. Uncertainty, not manipulation, of information seemed to dominate, always granted that many of these competing scientific and territorial interests would have tried to manipulate any definite information if they could. Information was not so much falsified or suppressed as hypothesized and 'accelerated', like electrons in the synchrotron itself, to divine some some essential element. In a negotiation, real information constitutes pressure. Here, as so often in governmental decision-making, the rival interests had to create what pressure they could from very little material.

In the end the German Government did not object to the breaking of the promise to Strasbourg and the possible move to Grenoble. Once the way was clear, President Mitterrand intervened and decreed in favour of Grenoble as an act of pork-barrel politics to help an old political friend who was running for re-election there. This autocratic action surprised many in Alsace, although such *ad hoc* presidential executive decisions are hardly unfamiliar in France (Comité de liaison 1984). They may even be suitable on scientific research questions where a 'rational' decision faces such adverse odds from the fragmented and opaque nature of the issues. Rigorous comparisons of the costs and benefits of different patterns of science policy spending or different proportions of the total budget going to science are not really to be had, so intractable and dynamic is the material to be reviewed. But a 'science policy' covering fundamental research must be maintained, however much it actually rests on guarded incrementalism, the ritualized movements between agencies, research boards, universities or colleges and other organized interests – all influenced by a definite 'hit parade' atmosphere encouraging intense competition and enthusiasms (and perhaps some cheating) to get into 'the charts' of official and popular esteem. This must all be rationalized and made intellectually respectable and this is the function of the shared rhetoric of unquestioned progress through science. Thus some superficial appearance of purpose and direction is given to the quest of the 'blind investor'.

Alsace (1985), *Contrat de plan 'Etat-Région Alsace'*.
Comité de liaison pour le Synchrotron (1984), *Le livre blanc d'un contrat rompu [The White Book of a Broken Contract]* (Strasbourg).
Comité scientifique (1982), *Report* (Paris: Ministry of Research and Technology).
European Science Foundation (1975), *Report* (Strasbourg).
European Science Foundation (1977), *Report of a working party: Synchrotron radiation – a perspective view for Europe*, November (Strasbourg).
European Science Foundation (1979), *Report: European Synchrotron Radiation Facility*, 4 vols: Feasibility Study; The Scientific Case; The Machine; The Instrumentation (Strasbourg).
Grenoble (1986), Conference on French ministerial cabinets, University of Social Sciences, Grenoble, 20 October.
Strasbourg (1983), *Contrat particulier de plan 'Strasbourg ville européenne'*, 24 November.
Tournon, Jean (1988), Les pressions publiques: les pouvoirs publiques sont le premier lobby de France [Public influence: the public authorities are France's principal lobby]; in *Jean Meynaud ou l'utopie revisitée [Jean Meynaud or the Utopian Dream Revisited]* (Lausanne), 172–200.

Eight

Conclusion
Science, Public Policy and the Authoritativeness of the Governmental Process

---

RICHARD TOPF

This Conclusion discusses further the concepts of 'perceived legitimacy' and 'policy community' featured in earlier chapters before raising the theme of post-materialist values and their relationship to governments' science-based policies and projects. Recent survey data from EC countries on public perceptions of science, technology and medicine are used for a final review of how these aspects of government and politics may be treated by increasingly post-materialist electorates in Western Europe. The politics of expert advice in these countries is likely to become more sophisticated and well-informed. It is, therefore, unlikely to lose any of its steadily increasing political saliency and academic interest.

SCIENCE IN MODERN SOCIETY

The world of the late twentieth century is dominated by science and technology. These twin pillars of the modern world have the capacity both for great good and for great harm ... Science casts a powerful spell over many citizens, and many policy makers, in contemporary democracies.

It is fitting that the editors of this volume should allude in their Introduction to Weber's seminal thesis of the disenchantment and intellectualization of the modern world and to the subsequent and still continuing debate about the extent to which science is merely a mystical re-enchantment (Whimster and Lash 1987). After all, Weber himself was quite clear about where science stood in the modern search for the Good Society. In a speech in 1918 he said:

I may leave aside altogether the naïve optimism in which science – that is, the technique of mastering life which rests upon science – has been celebrated as the way to happiness. Who believes in this? – aside from a few big children in university chairs or editorial offices (Weber 1948).

... Seventy years later, it is worth asking whether or not that naïve optimism still remains the comfort of Weber's big children, or may it be that the chapters in this volume show that science has remystified our larger society and scientific scepticism has become the burden of the intelligentsia? The significance which many contributors attach to the role of science and scientists in the process of legitimating public policy, while themselves emphasizing the lack of scientific certitude, at least suggests this.

As Saward points out in this volume, the notion of legitimation as commonly used by policy analysts refers to the perceived legitimacy of a policy, in the sense that policy-makers may claim credibility for the rationale of their policy formulation. That claim is then recognized by the wider society to whom the policy-makers are said to be accountable. Thus, the argument goes, when governments point to the role which scientific and technological expertise has played in the formulation of some policy, it follows that they believe this will demonstrate its authoritativeness, and hence add to its perceived legitimacy.

Clearly, we would expect there to be considerable variation in the applicability of this general thesis depending upon the policy field, the nature of the expertise, and so on. But an important underlying presupposition, implicit in the thesis, concerns the place of science and technology in Western political culture. *Pace* Weber, if policy makers are indeed to call upon science and technology to add to the perceived legitimacy of policy, then science and technology need to be positively evaluated by citizens, at least as the *means* to the Good Society and, better still, as valued ends in themselves.

Figure 8.1 Levels of public interest and information

	% claiming to be very interested				% claiming to be very well informed			
	GB	FR	PORT	FRG	GB	FR	PORT	FRG
New medical discoveries	43	61	26	32	11	23	6	10
New inventions and technology	37	48	21	19	12	18	5	10
New scientific discoveries	37	52	21	24	11	18	5	9
Sports in the news	23	25	28	27	21	17	21	24
New films	21	28	19	15	18	19	8	11
Politics	22	23	14	44	18	23	9	28

Source: Euro-barometer No. 31, 1989

Recent research in the European Communities (EC) into attitudes and beliefs about science throws some light on this (cf. Macgill in this volume). In the context of a comparative study of the perceived importance of science for society, representative samples throughout the EC were asked how interested and informed they were about a range of issues typically reported in the news. Figure 8.1 shows that in countries such as Great Britain and France with a tradition of prestigious scientific research, medical, technological and scientific discoveries were ranked first, second, and third as issues of interest to the population, well above such things as sport, cinema or politics. However, in other EC countries, such as Portugal, without such a tradition in recent times, the sciences do not head the rankings in the same way. West Germany, which at first sight we may have expected to be grouped with Britain and France, presents an interestingly anomalous case, for reasons to be considered later.

As noteworthy as levels of interest, however, is the finding that, in all countries, there is a very significant gap indeed between the percentage of their populations who declare themselves to be very interested in reading about medical or scientific matters and the much lower percentages who believe themselves to be well informed about these subjects. In Britain, for example, although some 40 per cent expressed great interest in medical and scientific discoveries, only just over 10 per cent believed themselves to be well informed. In France, where expressions of interest in medical and scientific subjects were the highest in the EC, the gap between interests and beliefs about being well informed ranged between 30 per cent and 45 per cent.

In other areas of potential interest such as sport, the cinema and politics, there were no similarly consistent gaps between levels of interest and belief about knowledge. Moreover, such subjective beliefs about levels of knowledge of scientific matters were belied by the results of a quiz about scientific knowledge included in the same survey. The results of this quiz showed that for countries such as Great Britain and France the population as a whole achieved a commendable mean of eight or more correct answers out of twelve questions.

Taken together, these findings could well be used as evidence in support of a remystification thesis, according to which scientific matters are of great interest to people even though they find them mystifying, to the extent that they under-estimate the extent of their own knowledge. Such a thesis has clear parallels with the blind investment argument discussed by Tournon in this volume.

However, the surveys also produced more direct evidence of the ambiguous feelings which people have about the role of science in society. Respondents were asked their views on a series of propositions about science, and Figure 8.2 gives some of the results. Britain and France again illustrate the dilemma. Well over three-quarters of their populations believe that scientific research should receive government support, and that science is improving the quality of life. Yet in Britain less than half, and in France just over half, believe that the benefits of science outweigh its harmful effects. Figure 8.2 shows similar, but less sharp, contradictions in public attitudes for Portugal and West Germany.

Thus in countries such as Britain and France, over three-quarters of the population believe that science improves the quality of life and should be supported by the State. About half that many say that they are very interested in scientific developments – still significantly more than those who express comparable levels

Figure 8.2   Public beliefs about science

	% agreeing			
	GB	FR	PORT	FRG
Even if it brings no immediate benefits, scientific research which advances the frontiers of knowledge should be supported by the government.	86	92	65	55
Science and technology are making our lives healthier, easier and more comfortable.	78	77	74	75
The benefits of science are greater than any harmful effects	44	59	59	36

Source: Euro-barometer No. 31, 1989

of interest in sport, films or politics. Yet just a small minority believe they are well informed about scientific matters.

It may well be, of course, that the instrumental value people place on science and technology is premised in part upon a combination of the positive images given in the mass media to high-technology medicine, such as heart transplants and whole-body scanners, and in part on their personal experience of the medium-level technology of domestic consumer products, such as dishwashers, video recorders and answering machines. We do not yet have the evidence to assess this one way or the other. Even were this the case, however, when taken together with public support for basic research, it must be concluded that science and technology continue to serve as powerful symbolic tools in the realm of political rhetoric (Edelman 1971).

A separate, comparative project of Britain and West Germany throws light on another aspect of mass orientations towards science in our political culture. This project was designed to examine Almond's and Verba's notion of the civic culture a full generation after their original work. In the late 1950s, Almond and Verba (1963) found that in Britain some 46 per cent of respondents named aspects of the political system as their main source of national pride, while just 7 per cent placed British scientific achievements first. In West Germany, 12 per cent placed scientific achievements first.

Figure 8.3 shows that by the late 1980s British scientific achievements were ranked second only to the monarchy as a source of national pride, with the welfare state in third place. Similarly in West Germany, although we noted that the population did not rank the sciences so highly among their interests, still German scientific achievements ran their welfare state a close fourth as a symbol of national pride.

We have no information about what in particular people had in mind when they expressed pride in scientific achievements. Again, however, it is clear that there are few indications of disillusionment with scientific achievements in general, and

Figure 8.3   Pride in national symbols

	% expressing pride			
	Great Britain		West Germany	
	1959	1987	1959	1987
Scientific achievements	7	59	12	37
British monarchy / German Basic Laws (1987/8) Any aspect of political and legal system (1959)	46	95	7	61
Welfare state	18	50	6	39
Economic achievements	10	16	33	50
Cultural achievements	6	20	11	21
Sporting achievements	< 1	32	2	21

Note: Overall responses may exceed 100% in multiple choices
Source: derived from Topf, Mohler and Heath 1989

'science' remains a potent symbol available to policy-makers seeking to legitimate their policies.

THE INTELLECTUALIZATION OF SOCIETY

It will be recalled that the naïve optimism referred to by Weber was precisely the belief that science could offer a way to happiness. Science, he argued, could offer training and clarity of thought and a 'technology of controlling life', but not life's meaning or a secular ethic (Whimster 1987). Not only may science be applied equally to great good or great harm, as this volume's editors attest, but it provides no values for distinguishing between them. Even to affirm the value of science and scientific progress themselves, Weber argued, is a value judgment which cannot be made on scientific grounds alone.

Of course, Weber saw the retreat of ultimate and most sublime values from the public realm as the fate of our times. It would follow from such a thesis that policy-makers would prefer to rely upon the culturally embedded authoritativeness of science – if such it is – to legitimate the means to achieving their policies, rather than to emphasize the values which underpin their ends – their vision of a good society.

Whether Weber was right in his empirical analysis of his time, and whether disenchantment prevails in our time, remain grand themes of debate well beyond the scope of this concluding chapter. None the less, there are specific areas of empirical research which bite more directly on science and public policy.

One of the better recognized recent challenges to disenchantment is the rise of a new religious fundamentalism in the West, led by the United States. For example, it is a matter for bemusement to many Europeans that some American school boards prohibit the teaching of Darwinian theories in their schools. Yet, within a subculture

Figure 8.4:   Acceptance of science

	% believing				
	GB	FR	FRG	PORT	USA
Human beings developed from earlier species of animals.	77	75	67	81	47
We depend too much on science and not enough on faith.	47	46	40	51	51

Sources: EC: Euro-barometer No.31, 1989; USA: Evans and Durant, 1989

where such a conventional scientific wisdom as evolution is rejected, it must be supposed that the scientist will carry less of an aura of authoritativeness by which to legitimate public policy than elsewhere.

The research project on understanding science in the European Communities asked people whether or not they believed in the central tenet of evolutionary theory: that human beings as we know them today developed from earlier species of animals. As Figure 8.4 illustrates, while in the United States less than 50 per cent of the population professed to believe in evolutionary theory, across EC countries from two-thirds to over three-quarters accepted it. In this respect, the populations of traditionally Roman Catholic countries, such as France, Italy, Portugal and Spain, proved to be no less convinced of Darwinian evolution than others, adding weight to the view of the American phenomenon as a post- or anti-Rationalist development.

Respondents were also asked if they agreed that we depend too much on science and not enough on faith. Given the highly positive attitudes towards the benefits bestowed by science and the support shown for basic research, we may have expected some crude confirmation of the disenchantment thesis, with science being seen as more dependable than faith. In fact, in most countries about half the population actually agreed with this statement, although in some, such as West Germany, as many as a third professed not to know one way or the other.

In this respect, therefore, it appears that, at the cultural level, we do find evidence that the disenchanting dominance of scientism may be under challenge. Again, we would need further evidence before we would be justified in interpreting these data as confirmation of any widely held view that more than science is necessary for the good life. Even so, the evidence so far suggests that, at least for half of several European populations, a crude appeal to the authoritativeness of science as a legitimation of policy may not always be enough.

SCIENCE AND POLICY LEGITIMATION

Analytically, it may be argued that issues enter on to the political agenda either pro-actively, because they were put there by a government or influential groups wishing to institute a deliberate programmeme, or reactively, in response to a perceived societal problem with which the existing routines of government are unable to cope (Topf 1992b). Clearly, in such a formulation the term perceived is being made to carry considerable analytical weight. Epidemics of food poisoning, which experts attribute to deficiencies in the regulation of agricultural or food processing safety standards, have a concrete and visible manifestation in the form of illness or death which may be perceived by the public at large. Even so, it should be noted that such perceptions require faith in, if not an understanding of, experts' diagnoses and their accounts of the causes of the epidemic.

In most of the cases presented in this volume, however, the perceptions of a problem are less direct. For example, even when the physical scale of a disaster at a nuclear installation becomes public knowledge, as it soon did in the case of Chernobyl, but did not at Sellafield (Liberatore and Macgill, in this volume), perceptions of the dangers of radiation are dependent solely upon expert opinion. Similarly, perceptions of the problems of chronic or progressive health complaints, especially when the cause is attributed to environmental conditions or diet (Mills 1992), are unlike problems arising from acute epidemics, in that the danger is intangible. In this sense, the problem is one perceived and defined by experts, not publics.

It is implicit in the application of theses about cultural demystification and remystification by science to analyses of policy legitimation that belief in science *per se* extends to scientists. Thus it is argued that governments seek to legitimate their policies in the eyes of mass publics by demonstrating that they have incorporated the authoritative advice of scientists. They do so, it is argued, because they assume that mass publics trust scientists.

Research into questions about public trust in public institutions and figures has long been a central feature of analyses of political culture. This research has shown that very often publics discriminate sharply between their beliefs in the values and ideals of the institutions and their trust in the individuals who comprise them. Publics may believe in democratic representation, but distrust politicians; they may believe in the rule of law, but distrust the police; and so on (Lipset and Schneider 1983; Jowell and Topf 1988). It would be equally possible, therefore, for publics to believe in the institution of science, but none the less to distrust the authoritativeness of the advice scientists give to policy-makers.

Figure 8.5:   Trust in scientists

	% believing scientists can be trusted to make the right decisions					
	FR	GB	FRG	ND	DEN	GR
Strongly agree	14	3	5	3	3	33
Agree	29	21	25	21	14	34
Neither agree nor disagree	30	16	37	19	18	23
Disagree	20	39	26	26	34	8
Strongly disagree	8	21	8	31	31	3

Source: Euro-barometer No.31, 1989

When European publics were asked directly if scientists could be trusted to make the right decisions, their responses varied considerably from country to country. Figure 8.5 gives some examples. They ranged from Denmark, where 65% said they could not, to Greece, where just 11 per cent said they could not. However, the Greek response was quite exceptional and, in seven out of twelve EC countries, less than 5% of respondents strongly agreed with the proposal that scientists could be trusted to make right decisions. Research into political culture has taught us that responses to decontextualised questions about trust should always be treated cautiously. Even so, the contrast between the widespread endorsement of scientific research and its societal benefits noted earlier and this pervasive expression of distrust of scientists as decision-makers could hardly be greater.

Of course the crucial issues for analyses of policy legitimation are whether levels of trust are changing over time, and whether they are reflected in the way people respond to policy proposals being advanced. It is not possible to tell from this cross-national survey conducted in 1989 if most Europeans have long distrusted scientists, or if the responses reflect people's more immediate reactions to the environmental and public health issues of the late 1980s, such as nuclear radiation fallout and food poisoning epidemics.

It is surely no coincidence, however, that such issues feature so prominently in this volume. Indeed, related aspects of the nuclear issue have been covered by no fewer than five contributors. All describe processes by which governments attempt to formulate policies using trans-scientific knowledge, against a background of a socially constructed reality which has increasingly become an alternative view of the risks of nuclear installations to that of the nuclear policy community. These accounts are, in effect, ones of the pro-nuclear community in retreat.

There can be little doubt that the Chernobyl disaster has served to strengthen this socially constructed reality. But this may well be because public consumption of some foodstuffs and water was prohibited on the basis of the scientists' criteria of potential risk to health, and because the name 'Chernobyl' has entered Western vocabularies as a symbol of nuclear disaster. No real disasters are known to have befallen the West so far as a result of 'Chernobyl'.

Still, we must be cautious of assigning too much weight to Chernobyl. In Britain, for example, Young's analysis of the social survey data suggests that perceptions of risk from nuclear power stations ran high throughout the 1980s, and that the Chernobyl disaster itself had no marked effect on such perceptions (Young 1988 76). In 1984, some 53% of British respondents thought it was very or quite likely that there would be a major accident at a British nuclear power station within ten years; immediately after Chernobyl, in 1986, this had risen to 59 per cent. Similarly in 1984, 87 per cent thought that waste from nuclear power stations presented a serious environmental hazard, rising to 90 per cent by 1986. Just 2 per cent of survey respondents did not have an opinion which they were prepared to express (*British Social Attitudes* survey 1987).

Thus, a range of survey evidence suggests that the British mass public, at least, shares few of the uncertainties about trans-science of the policy analysts expressed in this volume, or even of the scientists themselves. They know that nuclear waste is a serious hazard and that a nuclear accident is likely, and they place little faith in experts who tell them otherwise. It is in just such circumstances that the balance between perceived legitimacy and moral legitimacy, as Saward terms them, shifts decisively.

When we turn to public health issues, a comparison of the studies by Mills (1992) and by Street (1992) is illuminating. Mills focuses on the ability of a policy community to contain the issue of diet-related heart disease within existing governmental routines, by the manipulation of rival claims to authoritative knowledge advanced by different experts. Although Mills believes that this strategy of containment failed and the issue did enter on to the political agenda, he concludes that the resolution of the problem was against what is known to be in the best interests of public health.

Mills would, of course, concede that, within the terms of his own analysis, his is a value judgment. It is none the poorer for that. Explicitly, it is premised on the assumptions that the expert evidence of a weight of probabilities demonstrating a dietary link to heart disease is authoritative, and that this requires government to take regulatory measures beyond public education. Implicitly, there is at least the suggestion that a policy of public education is an inadequate one to meet the criterion of the public interest.

Public attitudes and beliefs about diet and health have been the subject of social surveys in Britain since the 1960s. Following the press publication of the NACNE findings which Mills discusses, the Health Education Council commissioned or funded a series of studies. The most recent available, from 1986, is reported in some detail by Sheiham, Marmot, Rawson and Ruck (1987) (three public health academics and a nutritionist, all of whom fall clearly into Mills's category of the policy community). These authors conclude, albeit with reservations, that trends in dietary attitudes and behaviour are clearly in the direction recommended by health professional and health educators (1987 111). However, they do not report clear evidence that such trends are the direct result of educative policies and, indeed, the evidence suggests that in many respects the mass public is aware of but confused about the links between diet and health.

Two specific findings illustrate the point for present purposes. First, with regard to heart disease, 70 per cent of survey respondents denied the fatalistic view that there is nothing one can to do to reduce the chances of getting it. Second, 73 per cent of respondents agreed, and just 11 per cent disagreed, with the statement that experts contradict each other over what makes a healthy diet (Sheiham *et al.* 1987 98). Thus, public beliefs about diet and health are reminiscent of those about science and technology generally – interested, not well informed, and with no public perception of an issue requiring new government policy, whatever may be the views within the policy community itself.

Street's account of the development of a British policy towards AIDS parallels that of Mills in several respects. In this case, too, the perception of the issue is entirely dependent upon the acceptance of the authoritativeness of expert knowledge, which has both constructed AIDS and produced its prognosis. In this volume, both the Introduction and the chapter by Saward have reviewed in some detail the issues in the sociology of knowledge raised by this social constructionist usage of knowledge creation. Two points of elaboration are sufficient here.

Firstly, within the scientific community itself, the virus account of AIDS does not go unchallenged. Secondly, while the horrific effects on individual people of some killing condition are clear enough for all to see, it remains the case that the societal effects of AIDS throughout the West are statistically insignificant, when measured in terms of overall morbidity and mortality rates. In Britain, for example, since reporting began in 1982 there has been a total of under 4,400 reported cases of AIDS; some 2,500 of these are known to have died *(Communicable Disease Report*, 1991). By no normal convention could the spread of a disease at this rate be called an epidemic which required action by government.

From this perspective, therefore, AIDS is akin to the diet and health issue in that the perception of the problem depends upon its definition by a policy community of experts. It differs only in the respect that the AIDS policy community could be said to have been more successful. Street's account, after all, may be interpreted as one of the effective routinization of an issue, with little public controversy over government policy, despite frequent and often scare-mongering media coverage being given to AIDS.

Survey evidence again reflects public interest and confusion. In Britain, some 60 per cent of people believe that, within the next five years, AIDS will cause more deaths in Britain than any other single disease, and a further 27 per cent believe that this view is only slightly exaggerated. This pessimism is of a different order of magnitude from that of the policy community itself. At the same time, just a third (34 per cent) of the population believe that a vaccine will be discovered within five years, and almost half (45 per cent) say they do not know.

On the question of who is to blame, which Street raises, some 57 per cent of British people believe that AIDS sufferers have only themselves to blame but, at the same time, 60 per cent believe sufferers deserve more sympathy. While public perceptions of the AIDS risk are in line with conventional scientific views of its correlation with sexual behaviour, two-thirds of the general public profess to believing that even occasional, heterosexual, extra-marital sex carries with it considerable risk of contracting AIDS (Brook 1988).

It would be rash to speculate on why it is that the AIDS policy community seems to have been so much more successful than the diet and health community in promoting its account of social reality, given the lack of hard scientific data in both cases. As Street points out, media coverage of AIDS victims, especially when associated with the royal family, doubtless has helped to make images of the risks more concrete. But if the outcome of the educational dimension of government policy may be seen, from the scientific perspective, as an exaggerated view of reality, how has this affected the other two dimensions of policy – patient care and research – both of which directly involve the scientific community?

The survey data suggest that the British public does not have views one way or the other about directing more resources into care of those dying from AIDS, with just 8 per cent feeling strongly that this is necessary (and 5 per cent strongly that it is not). However, 50 per cent have strong views about resources for more research, these being 2 to 1 in favour (Brook 1988 81). Such attitudes, which are in line with general public evaluations of science and the particular ambivalence about the moral aspects of AIDS, would seem to demonstrate the perceived legitimacy of the current policies which Street describes, while reinforcing the scientific perspective.

POLICY LEGITIMATION AND THE MORAL ORDER

Weber's disenchantment thesis is important for the general insights it gives into both the perceived legitimacy which the authoritativeness of science has tradition-ally bestowed upon public policy in modern societies and the dangers which may develop when the instrumental rationality of science is transmuted into a value rationality in its own right. The social survey evidence reviewed here suggests that European mass publics continue to have faith in science *per se*, whatever may be the conventional wisdom among post-Kuhnian academics, but they have little in scientists themselves as decision-makers.

Inglehart's post-materialism thesis builds upon Weber's by suggesting that there is in process an inter-generational culture shift in Western societies (Inglehart 1977, 1990). This shift away from materialist values towards post-materialist ones, he argues, is partly caused by the improvements to the material conditions in post-war societies which science and technology have brought about. Thus change has been most rapid in those societies, such as West Germany, which have experienced the greatest post-war improvements in societal security and prosperity. But, important-ly, such changes embody a reaction against the disenchanted values of materialism which fostered those societal changes in the first place.

At a general level, therefore, the post-materialism thesis suggests a decisive break from the pro-science evaluations of disenchantment, illustrated by the survey responses we have considered. In his most recent version of an evolving analysis, Inglehart writes (1990 268–69):

> For Materialists ... highly developed science and industry symbolize progress and prosperity. Among Postmaterialists ... big business, big science, and big government [are] bureaucratic organizations that are evaluated negatively because they are inherently impersonal and hierarchical, minimizing individual self-expression and human contact.

The nature of the explanation which Inglehart offers for differences between the positive, materialist evaluations of science and the negative post-materialist ones is important. Materialists value science for the concrete economic benefits it may be believed to have brought, and for the future benefits it symbolizes. On the other hand, post-materialists reject the societal processes inherent in the institutionalized forms taken by big science, rather than the perceived benefits of science as such. At this level, therefore, room could probably still be found for big science in a post-materialist society, were the organizational structures open to 'democratization'.

The results of the EC survey offer strong evidence in support of Inglehart's thesis. We already noted from Figure 8.1 that, in the case of West Germany, the exemplar of an evolving post-materialist culture, attitudes towards the sciences were atypical and ambivalent. When we compare the views of these German materialists with post-materialists, these ambiguities are highlighted. Post-materialists are somewhat more in favour than materialists of state-supported basic research (62 per cent to 51 per cent), but they are markedly less convinced that the benefits of science outweigh the harmful effects (28 per cent to 45 per cent). Perhaps most telling of all, German post-materialists are four times more distrustful of scientists than are materialists. Just 13 per cent of post-materialists agree that scientists can be trusted at all to make right decisions, compared with 52 per cent of materialists.

There is another, related, element to post-materialism, however, which may have equally fundamental implications for the process of policy legitimation. Post-materialists are both much more likely to be politically active citizens than materialists and to value the process of democratic participation in policy-making as a good in its own right (Dalton 1988; Inglehart 1990). Indeed, they are likely to value a policy proposal with a democratic and participative, formulative process more than they do a policy proposal which emphasizes the instrumentally rational achievement of specific ends. In other words, for post-materialists policy-making is not simply about finding the best solution to a problem. The ends do not always justify the means (Weber 1948).

One consequence of this participatory revolution is that it shifts the balance of authoritativeness of the inputs into the policy process away from expertise, and towards democratic representation. In situations where there is a clash of world views between the expert and the affected layman, post-materialists may well value the views of the lay citizen above those of the scientist.

Such a shift has particular implications for policy processes where the policy makers' goal is problem-solving, rather than the advancement of an ideological programmeme (Topf 1992). It means, for example, that when there is public concern over the dangers of radiation, or AIDS, or outbreaks of food poisoning, post-materialists will favour a policy which effectively takes into account and responds to public perceptions of the problem, even if such perceptions go against expert opinion. This is partly because post-materialists are suspicious of the authoritativeness of charismatic, institutionalized expertise, precisely because of the exclusivity of such expertise, identified in the Introduction. But it is partly also because post-materialists attach less weight to scientifically accurate answers – even when the experts may be shown to have been correct – than to the appropriate policy-formulating process (Barker 1992b).

Moreover, in many countries there is a close connection between the emergence of post-materialism and the rise of new social movements such as those concerned with ecology, nuclear power or nuclear weapons (Inglehart 1990). Thus a culture shift arising from the emergence of post-materialism is held to contribute to traditional political agendas changing towards the so-called new politics of environmentalism, public health, peace movements, minority rights and so on. In other words, there is a direct relationship between the emergence of specific, trans-scientific issues on the political agenda, on the one hand, and of politically skilled and active citizens who are likely to question the authoritativeness of Establishment-expertise, on the other.

It is perhaps no coincidence, therefore, that all of the substantive policy areas reviewed in this volume fall within the broad domain of the new politics agenda – nuclear power, public health, and environmental planning. We have seen that, overwhelmingly, mass publics remain pro-science. They profess to be more interested in scientific and technological issues than they are in sport, or cinema! They believe science and technology have created a better way of life, and they favour government support for further research which advances the frontiers of knowledge, even if this brings no immediate benefits.

However, recent theories of shifts in political culture point to structural and inter-generational changes over time within societies (Inglehart 1990; cf. Heath and Topf 1987, Topf 1989, 1991). These theories identify education as a key indicator of changes in belief and value systems within societies. They argue, albeit on differing analytical premises, that post-industrial societies are undergoing a process of cultural change involving value systems which affect the traditional bases of policy legitimation.

We have noted already that Inglehart associates the rise of post-materialism with the new political agenda. But post-materialists are more likely than materialists, not only to bring into question conventional, institutional, policy processes, such as expert commissions and inquiries by which governments seek to legitimate their policies, but also the explicit or implicit value assumptions of the policies themselves. In the areas of the new political agenda, this means that post-materialists are likely to challenge the moral legitimacy of arguments which, for example, attempt to justify the development of nuclear power on economic grounds, or the unchecked usage of road vehicles on the grounds that they are more efficient and economical than rail or water transport.

So far as the place of expert advice in the policy process is concerned, it would appear that in post-industrial societies there may be emerging a type of politically participative citizen who holds a world view within which political participation is regarded as a political obligation and a moral good. These citizens are well-educated, take an interest in science and technology, and are usually well informed about developments. They support basic research for its own sake as a contribution to human knowledge, but they are not among Weber's big children who see science as a way to the good society. They are likely to bring their own values and moral judgments to bear most on those areas of policy where the trans-scientific nature of the issue makes the authoritative legitimation of that policy most vulnerable to criticism from knowledgeable outsiders. Doubtless to the chagrin of politicians for whom the authoritativeness of expertise is a convenient veil for the retreat from ultimate values, the indications are that the new active citizens may make a bid to take the fate of our times into their own hands.

116   RICHARD TOPF

Almond, G.A. and Verba, S. (1963), *The Civic Culture: Political attitudes and democracy in five nations* (Princeton, NJ: Princeton University Press).
Barker, A. (1992), Professionalised expertise and the politics of British land-use planning; in Peters, B.G. and Barker, A. (eds), *op. cit.*
British Social Attitudes surveys (1984–90), [annual social surveys conducted by Social and Community Planning Research, and deposited in the ESRC Data Archive, University of Essex, Colchester, England].
Brook, L. (1988), The public's response to AIDS; in Jowell, R. *et al.* (eds), *op. cit.*
Communicable Disease Report, 1991, Public Health Laboratories Series, vol.1:10 (Colindale: Communicable Disease Surveillance Centre).
Dalton, R.J. (1988), *Citizen Politics in Western Democracies* (Chatham, NJ: Chatham House).
Edelman, M. (1971), *Politics as Symbolic Action: Mass arousal and quiescence* (Chicago, IL: Markham).
Euro-barometer No. 31 (1989), [European Communities social survey directed by K. Reif, and deposited in the Cologne Data Archive, Germany].
Evans, G. and Durant, J. (1989), Understanding of science in Britain and the USA; in Jowell, R. *et al.* (eds), *op. cit.*
Heath, A.F. and Topf, R.G. (1987), Political culture; in Jowell, R. *et al.* (eds), *op. cit.*
Inglehart, R. (1977), *The Silent Revolution: Changing values and political styles among Western publics* (Princeton, NJ: Princeton University Press).
Inglehart, R. (1990), *Culture Shift in Advanced Democracies* (Princeton, NJ: Princeton University Press).
Jowell, R. and Topf, R.G. (1988), Trust in the Establishment; in Jowell, R. *et al.* (eds), *op. cit.*
Jowell R., Witherspoon S. and Brook, L. (eds), (1987), *British Social Attitudes: The 1987 Report* (Aldershot: Gower).
Jowell, R., Witherspoon, S. and Brook, L. (eds), (1988), *British Social Attitudes: The 5th Report* (Aldershot: Gower).
Jowell, R., Witherspoon, S. and Brook, L. (eds), (1989), *British Social Attitudes: Special international report* (Aldershot: Gower).
Lipset, S.M. and Schneider, W. (1983), *The Confidence Gap: Business, labor and government in the public mind* (New York: The Free Press).
Mills, M. (1992), Expert policy advice to the British government on diet and heart disease; in Peters, B.G. and Barker, A. (eds), *op. cit.*
Peters, B.G. and Barker, A . (eds), (1992), *Advising West European Governments: Inquiries, Expertise and Public Policy* (Edinburgh: Edinburgh University Press).
Sheiham, S., Marmot, M., Rawson, D. and Ruck, N. (1987), Food values: health and diet; in Jowell, R. *et al.* (eds), *op. cit.*
Street, J. (1992), Policy advice in an established official advice structure: AIDS advice through the British Department of Health; in Peters, B.G. and Barker, A. (eds), *op. cit.*
Topf, R.G. (1989), Political culture and political change in Britain, 1959–87; in Gibbins, J. (ed.) *Contemporary Political Culture: Politics in a postmodern age* (London: Sage).
Topf, R.G. (1991), The moral order of the nation-state: mapping values, collective identities, and citizenship; in Klages, H., Hippler, H.J. and Herbert, W. (eds), *Werte und Wandel: Ergebnisse und Methoden einer Forschungstradition [Values and Change: Findings and methods of a research tradition]*.
Topf, R.G. (1992), Advice to Governments: some theoretical and practical issues; in Peters, B.G. and Barker, A. (eds), *op. cit.*
Topf, R.G., Mohler, P. Ph., and Heath, A.F. (1989), Pride in one's country: Britain and West Germany; in Jowell, R. *et als.* (eds), *op. cit.*
Weber, M. (1948), Science as a vocation; in Gerth, H.H. and Mills, C.W. (eds), *From Max Weber* (London: Routledge & Kegan Paul).

Whimster, S. (1987), The secular ethic and the cult of modernism; in Whimster, S. and Lash, S. (eds), *op. cit.*

Whimster, S. and Lash, S. (eds), (1987), *Max Weber: Rationality and modernity* (London: Allen & Unwin).

Young, K. (1988), Interim report: rural prospect; in Jowell, R. *et al.* (eds), *op. cit.*

A Note on B. Guy Peters and Anthony Barker (eds), *Advising West European Governments: Inquiries, Expertise and Public Policy* (Edinburgh: Edinburgh University Press 1992)

This book contains the following chapters:

1. THE EDITORS (University of Pittsburgh and University of Essex)
   Introduction: governments, information, advice and policy-making
   Aided by figures, the introduction asks what are the problems faced by a government seeking usable and authoritative policy advice based on sound research findings or other information. Many pitfalls are discussed including the temptation to shape a policy problem around the type and the limited quantity of the information available instead of expanding the supply of suitable information for relevant advice. Governments are uniquely equipped to 'mandate' (or themselves create) new information and advice, for example through contracts with scientists and R & D laboratories.

2. ANTHONY BARKER (University of Essex)
   Patterns of decision advice processes: a review of types and a commentary on some recent British practices
   This chapter carries the review of official commissions and committees into wider and newer policy territory to show just how many forms and *modus operandi* for advice-giving to governments in advanced societies there may now be. In particular, catastrophic accidents and perceived official failures are increasingly expected to yield a 'public inquiry', to reveal the 'truth' and also satisfy concern and criticism by its rituals and legitimation processes. A 'hierarchy' of types of official inquiries and reports available to governments is offered. Again, all advanced political systems have something similar, so this chapter is not solely British in its application.

3. MARTIN BULMER (London School of Economics and Political Science)
The Royal Commission and Departmental Committee in the British policy- making process

These two long-established, high status and general purpose British devices for official advice on policy are reviewed by this subject's leading exponent. All developed political systems maintain a similar form for major issues or for special (including catastrophic or scandalous) events

4. PIERRE CHABAL (European University Institute, Florence)
Advice-giving, time constraints and ministerial efficiency

As a conscious contrast to the other chapters, this comparative review of government ministers' efficiency concentrates on the business of their receiving expert advice and information, whether *via* their civil servants, political advisers or political colleagues in the legislature. The dominant constraint is their lack of time and the main lesson for advisers is to present advice in the most usable and relevant form. May 'objective' advice-giving be twisted and damaged by such practical and political imperatives?

5. FRANS LEEUW (Netherlands Court of Audit)
Analysing policy theories and the systematic use of knowledge for public policy

A Dutch civil service policy analyst sets out the method of comprehensive literature search to establish 'best practice' ('state of the art') in a policy field and applies it to an actual Dutch policy-making exercise to combat juvenile delinquency. The theoretical social science context of such systematic discovery work is described.

6. OTTO SINGER (University of Konstanz)
Knowledge and politics in economic policy-making: official economic advisers in the USA, Great Britain and Germany

Taking economics as the allegedly most scientifically developed of the social sciences, this chapter reviews the three countries' established systems for technical economic advice. Their fortunes throughout the Keynesian policy 'collapse' (and possible current revival) are traced, with considerable benefit to the understanding of German, British and American policy-making in this field.

7. AXEL MURSWIECK (University of Heidelberg)
Policy advice and decision-making in the German federal bureaucracy

The prominent formal role of institutionalized expert advice-giving in the Bonn system is outlined: its symbolic nature is also described. The case of expert recommendations on drug safety is presented with USA comparisons.

8. ANDREAS LANGMANN (Ruhr University of Bochum)
Policy advice on rearranging the North – South relationship: the fortunes of the Pearson, Tinbergen (RIO project) and Brandt Commissions 1968–80
This chapter deals with three quasi-official international advisory commissions of great importance for West European governments. It brings a valuable extra dimension to the book's theme.

9. MICHAEL MILLS (City of London Polytechnic)
Expert policy advice to the British government on diet and heart disease
Government health programmes – whether concerned to discourage alcohol and tobacco or to promote more healthy eating and exercise – rely squarely on medical and scientific advice. They are also heavily lobbied by the producers to curb regulatory pressures on their operations and profits. This case study of contrary pressures on the British government to be either more or less active on diet and heart disease programmes emphasizes the relative strength of one Government Department (Agriculture) compared with another (Health) on this shared policy problem. A 'policy community' explanation is offered in which 'food production' appears to outrank 'public health'.

10. WOLFGANG HOFFMANN-RIEM (Hans Bredow Institut für Rundfunk und Fernsehen, University of Hamburg)
Media politics and policy research in Germany: a precarious relationship
This is an account of how expert information and advice was manipulated or even abused during a powerful political pressures to introduce commercial sponsored broadcasting, cable systems and new telecommunications into Germany. A legislative committee of inquiry (enquête-kommission) features in this cautionary analysis.

11. ROGER WILLIAMS (University of Manchester)
The House of Lords Select Committee on science and technology within British Science policy and the nature of science policy advice
The special problems of policy advice in science and technology fields are reviewed here, against a general and theoretical context. The work of the largely scientifically expert legislative committee in question is then outlined as an example of both the receiving and offering of science policy advice. (Professor Williams holds a chair in science policy studies and is an official adviser of this House of Lords committee).

12. JOHN STREET (University of East Anglia)
Policy advice in an established official advice structure: AIDS advice through the British Department of Health
When a novel issue or challenge arises, the relevant policy advice provided to, or sought by, governments will be shaped by the existing policy advice structure – even though this may be inappropriate and may even delay the advice

which governments actually need on that subject. The author applies this common pathology of official advice-giving to the first years of AIDS advice to the government from its established medical advisers. Advice on relevant human sexual behaviour was therefore neglected, despite its central role in actual anti-AIDS programmes.

13. ANTHONY BARKER (University of Essex)
Professionalized expertise and the politics of British land-use planning
  Much of the scientific and technical advice to the British government on land-use planning is (unusually and even uniquely) presented *via* an elaborate system of public inquiries (hearings) where rival experts have usually been cross-examined by rival advocates. This professional expertise is, therefore, processed into a quasi-judicialized form and this, the author maintains, limits the normal policy initiative open to the government in most other policy fields. This chapter is, therefore, a study of how process and procedure may affect what scientific or technical advice the government receives and what it can do with it.

14. RICHARD TOPF (City of London Polytechnic and Nuffield College, Oxford)
Conclusion: advice to Governments – some theoretical and practical issues
  This overview chapter recommends a State-centred perspective for devising a typology which furthers the analysis of advice to governments and the advisers who provide it. In the advanced, increasingly post-industrial societies, the state becomes an integrated and rational 'system' with 'functions' (in organization theory terms). It can rely for its continuing stability on its vertical integration as its responsibilities and operations continue to increase. The consequences for the policy adviser, policy analyst and policy-maker of the increasing penetration of society by this type of integrated, rational State are outlined.

Index of Names

Almond, G., 106, 116
Altissimo, R., 39
Aubert, J.F., 50, 59
Barker, A., 12, 15, 114
Barker, C.J., 67, 72
Barnes, B., 18, 30
Barnes, M., 88
Bijker, W.E., 27, 30
Black, Sir D., 65–6, 71
Blowers, A., 79, 89
Brickman, R., 35, 46
Brook, L., 113, 116
Bupp, I.C., 21, 24, 28, 30

Cartwrigt, Dr., 62
Collingridge, D., 13, 15, 26
Collins, H., 18–19, 26, 30
Conrad, J., 18, 30
Crouch, D., 65, 72

Dalton, R., 114, 116
Derby, S.L., 30
Derian, J.C., 21, 24, 28, 30
De Sanctis, V., 40, 46
Divine, R.A., 20, 30
Douglas, M., 6, 15
Downs, A., 8, 15
Dror, Y., 4, 15
Dunn, W.N., 8, 15
Durant, J., 108, 116
Edelman, M., 106, 116
Edge, D., 18, 30
Eisenbud, E., 63, 72

Evans, G., 108, 116

Fallows, S., 20, 30
Fernandez, A., 29, 32
Fernie, J., 85, 90
Fischer, F., 5, 7, 15
Fischoff, B., 29–30
Fleck, Sir A., 78, 90
Flowers, Lord, 79
Ford, D., 22–3, 31
Frutiger, A., 50, 59
Funtowicz, S.O., 66, 68–9, 72
Gardner, M., 61–2
Germann, R., 46, 50, 53, 59
Gerth, H.H., 116
Goddard, S., 89
Gofman, J., 20, 31
Goggin, M., 12, 15
Gorz, A., 51, 59
Gould, P., 33, 46
Gowing, M., 77–8, 90
Goyder, J., 79, 90
Grimston, M., 62, 72
Grove, J.W., 5, 15
Guedeney, C., 29, 31

Hafele, W., 25–7, 31
Hall, T., 75, 78–9, 90
Hamlin, C., 81, 90
Heath, A.F., 106, 115–16
Herbert, W., 116
Hippel, F. van, 23, 31
Hippler, H.J., 116

Subject Index

Acid rain, 29
Advisory Board for the Research Councils (UK),
  13
AIDS policy, 7–8, 111–14
'ALRA'/'ALARP', 82–3, 87–8

Bhopal disaster, 19
British Nuclear Fuels PLC (BNFL) (UK), 79–81,
  84–6
Central Electricity Generating Board (UK), 80,
  82–9 passim
Centre National de la Récherche Scientifique
  (France), 95, 101
Challenger disaster, 19
Chernobyl disaster, 19, 33–47, 109–10
Committee for Global Energy Conception
  (Swiss), 52–5
Committee for Revision of Atomic Law (Swiss),
  55–8
Committee on Medical Aspects of Radiation
  (UK), 64
Council of States (Swiss), 50

Darwinian public beliefs, 107–8
Department of Education and Science (UK), 13
'End of ideology' theory, 49–50
ENEA (National Committee for Nuclear and
  Alternative Energy) (Italy), 35–44 passim
ENEL (State electricity utility) (Italy), 35–7
European Science Foundation, 91–2, 96–8, 101
Expert scientists in science policy-making:
  advisory committees of, 12, 52–8, 64, 66–7,
  70–1, 95–6

as policy dissenters, 17–30 passim, 42–3
as single government science adviser, 12–13
'closure' of scientific disputes, 18–19, 24
in 'pathfinder' technologies, 25–30, passim
legitimation of policy by, 10, 12, 18, 35, 42
location in organisations of, 9, 11–13, 26–30,
  95–6
location in scientific discovery process of, 18–
  30, 95–6
networks and policy communities of, 10, 13,
  64–71, 96–8, 100, 111–13
peer control and consensus among, 13, 17–30,
  64, 75, 94, 96–8
public trust in, 109–13
relation to mass media of, 42–6
sources of scientific uncertainty among, 17–30
  passim, 42–4, 61–71
vested interests as expert advisers, 95

Federal Council (Swiss), 50
Fleck reports on the Windscale fire of 1957, 78
food safety issues, 6
Freedom of Information Act (USA), 23
Friends of the Earth (UK), 79, 83

General Electric (USA), 20
government officials as expert advisers, 12–13
greenhouse effect, 29

Health and Safety Executive (and Commission)
  (UK), 74–5, 88
health care management, 1–4
Health Education Council (UK), 111